GREAT STEAM
LOCOMOTIVES
OF ALL TIME

GREAT STEAM LOCOMOTIVES OF ALL TIME

O. S. NOCK

ILLUSTRATED BY
CLIFFORD & WENDY MEADWAY

ARCO PUBLISHING COMPANY, INC.
New York

Published 1977 by Arco Publishing Company, Inc.
219 Park Avenue South, New York, N.Y. 10003

Copyright © Blandford Press Ltd 1976

Printed in Great Britain

Library of Congress Cataloging in Publication Data

Nock, Oswald Stevens.

   Great steam locomotives of all time.
   Includes index.
   1. Locomotives.   I. Title.
TJ605.N6 625.2'61'09 76-56418
ISBN 0-668-04209-5
ISBN 0-668-04250-8 pbk.

CONTENTS

PREFACE

When the Blandford Press asked me to choose sixty-four steam locomotives from the railways of the world to form a 'gallery of fame', of all the 150 years from the opening of the Stockton and Darlington Railway to the present time, the question arose as to what constituted a 'famous', or a 'great', locomotive. There are certainly quite a lot from which to choose! Furthermore, this new book as planned was not to be purely a collection of pictures with simple explanatory captions. It was to present a connected theme, revealing something of the interplay of design practice, and the sharing of experience by engineers in many different parts of the world. So within the parameter of 'sixty-four' we had to bring in many overseas railways, and inevitably examples from some of the best-known countries such as Great Britain, France, and the U.S.A. had to be strictly rationed. Again fame and greatness are not necessarily the same thing. A very famous engine like, for example, the *City of Truro*, did not in retrospect contribute a great deal towards the world development of locomotive practice, while others perhaps not so well known unquestionably rank among the 'great'.

So the title was chosen with some deliberation. At the same time it must be emphasised that the selected 'sixty-four' were of my own personal choice. Those who have studied locomotive history may not agree that some of these choices were justified. In a field of such intense and ever-growing interest, partisan feelings often run high, and not only among British enthusiasts. But I have endeavoured to spread the interest as widely and impartially as I can. In one respect, however, I venture to think that all readers will be agreed, and that is upon the superb quality of the portraits of the locomotives that have been painted by my friends Clifford and Wendy Meadway.

O. S. NOCK

HISTORICAL
BACKGROUND

Even with the scholarship of J. G. H. Warren, Ahrons, C. F. Dendy-Marshall and others at one's elbow, it is at times difficult to conjure up a true picture of the conditions in which men of humble birth and little education created the steam locomotive from virtually nothing, and in a mere twenty-five years had developed and incorporated all the basic features that were to make it the simplest, cheapest, and most reliable form of railway motive power that has yet been devised. I have the greatest admiration for some of the latest diesel and electric locomotives, and of the wonderfully ingenious features of design built into them. But they are complicated, they are expensive, and – 'tell it not in Gath' – they *do* go wrong. One can turn to an American historian of our own times, John H. White, Jr., who, has written:

> 'It was the British who perfected the basic design of the loco-motive and introduced the separate firebox, multitubular boiler, direct connection to the wheels, blast pipe and other fundamental features that remained with the steam locomotive to the end of its production. American improvements – mainly in running gears – were hardly as fundamental or as far-reaching as the work of the British designers, who had perfected their basic design by 1830.'

The *Rocket*, winner of the Rainhill Trials in 1829, and the first locomotive to incorporate all the features enumerated by Mr. White, stands head and shoulders over everything that had gone before, as the first truly great locomotive of all time.

Although importing many British locomotives in early days, the Americans quickly found that the short wheelbases and rigid-frame construction of Stephenson's basic designs took unkindly to their own railroads. At the beginning of the railway age the U.S.A. was largely a rural nation, with little capacity for large capital invest-ment; and in contrast to contemporary conditions in England, where manufacturing centres that had grown up during the Industrial Revolution, urgently needed better communications. The American railways had to be built as cheaply as possible, because at first speed was quite a secondary consideration. The first railroads included steep gradients, much severe curvature, and track that was lightly laid, often with little more anchorage than laying the sleepers, or 'ties' as they are known in North America, on the surface of the ground. To meet these conditions American engineers developed locomotives with a more flexible wheelbase and suspension; and while British railways were using relatively short six-wheelers of the 2–2–2 and 2–4–0 types, with little lateral play in any of the axles, the Americans introduced locomotives with four-wheeled swivelling trucks or bogies that would respond easily to the curves and inequalities in the road. When four-coupled driving wheels were combined with a leading bogie the classic 'American' 4–4–0 was produced – so 'great' a locomotive type of all time that for many decades it was virtually the standard type for every kind of work in North America.

In England the quest of speed became a major consideration before the 1830s were out. On Brunel's strong recommendation the Great Western Railway struck out on a much bolder course than George Stephenson was following. The great pioneer of the north had built the Stockton and Darlington Railway to the same rail gauge as that of the old colliery lines, 4 ft. 8½ in., and the Liverpool and Manchester, the London and Birmingham, and others were built similarly on the confident assumption that they would all be linked up in a national network one day. But Brunel and the Great Western Railway settled for the 7 ft. gauge, and it was perhaps ironical that its astonishing possibilities for high speed were soon being demonstrated by locomotives that were a direct development of one of Robert Stephenson's basic designs – the 2–2–2 'Patentee' of 1834, with inside cylinders, for the Liverpool and Manchester Railway. Brunel's brilliant locomotive superintendent, Daniel Gooch, had a Stephenson-built 2–2–2, the *North Star*, bought up secondhand, and from experience with this he designed his famous 'Firefly' class; and what those engines did in the 1840s certainly entitles them to their place in the gallery of fame.

As the speeds attained on the early railways began to leap up, and maxima of 60 m.p.h. were being attained no more than twenty years

2

after the opening of the Stockton and Darlington Railway, difficulties with rolling, swaying and other undesirable accompaniments of travel began to arise. The demands upon locomotive power were increasing, and larger boilers were needed, and as these had to be located clear of the driving axles, they went higher above the rails, and led to swaying and rolling at speed. On the Great Western Gooch had no difficulties in this respect, because the wider gauge gave greater lateral stability. It was, however, one of Gooch's assistants, T. R. Crampton by name, who invented a form of locomotive to overcome this risk of instability. He put a single pair of driving wheels at the extreme rear end, so that a large boiler could be mounted, with a relatively low centre line, over the carrying rather than the driving wheels. The result was an extraordinary, and highly picturesque locomotive. Relatively few of them were built for service in Great Britain, but the type became extremely popular in France, and they became the standard type of express locomotive on the Northern, Eastern, and on the Paris, Lyons and Mediterranean Railways. They were also used on some of the old individual State railways of Germany. No French railwayman would dispute the idea that the Crampton was one of the 'great' locomotives of all time.

In Great Britain the 2–4–0 type became one of the most popular types of express passenger locomotive during the mid, and latter part of the nineteenth century. On some railways there was some preference for the 2–2–2, as it was thought that a single pair of driving wheels would give greater freedom in running for an express engine; but with improved constructional methods, harder materials, and a better understanding of the science of lubrication the 2–4–0 could be made to run equally fast, while having a superior factor of adhesion, and ability to accelerate a load more rapidly from rest. Three railways concerned with heavy and competitive traffic between England and Scotland, the London and North Western, the Midland, and the North Eastern were extensive users of the 2–4–0 type, and examples from each of these companies have happily been preserved. Each of them would qualify for inclusion among the 'greats', especially *Hardwicke* of the L. & N.W.R., which made the record run from Crewe to Carlisle at an average speed of 67 m.p.h. in the 1895 'Race to the North'. Equally, the Midland 2–4–0 preserved is the work of

Matthew Kirtley, who sponsored the development of a design feature that was almost as fundamental as some of those incorporated in the *Rocket*, namely the brick arch in the firebox, which made practicable the economic burning of coal, instead of coke. But there are even brighter 'stars' than the 2–4–0s to represent the L. & N.W.R. and the Midland, and this has left the North Eastern in this field – and very magnificently too.

The French railways in their early days built many locomotives of the so-called 'long boiler' type – another patented design of Robert Stephenson's. The idea was that a long boiler barrel promoted more complete combustion of the fuel, and thus more economical working. This worked out very well so far as the boiler was concerned, but the wheels were grouped on a relatively short wheelbase, with all the axles ahead of the firebox, so as to permit of a deep grate, on which a thick fire could be maintained. But that short wheelbase gave rise to a yawing action at speed that sometimes led to derailments. In Great Britain development of the 'long-boilered' type was confined to freight locomotives, notable on the Stockton and Darlington line. In France, however, the slower speed of travel, which in some areas favoured the 'stern-wheeler' Cramptons, led to a continuance of the long-boilered type for passenger work. A different kind of instability seemed to affect the French 2–4–0s, that of fore-and-aft pitching, and they changed the 2–4–0 into the 2–4–2, to provide additional support at the rear end. This became the standard express passenger type on the Paris, Lyons and Mediterranean Railway, but its greatest success was on the Paris–Orleans line.

Back to England, the work of William Stroudley on the London Brighton and South Coast Railway had for a time an almost worldwide influence. He was a master of detail, a perfectionist in manufacture, and a man who had a talent for artistic elegance in the external, or aesthetic, form of his locomotives. His precepts must, however, be studied in the light of running conditions on the Brighton Railway. When he became locomotive superintendent the 2–2–2 was the standard type for passenger work. But faced with the need for a more powerful type he adopted the 0–4–2 rather than the 2–4–0 wheel arrangement, and his 'Gladstone' class made a remarkable name for themselves, albeit in a train service that was not then very fast. He advocated use of the 'front-coupled' type on the grounds that the large leading wheels enabled an engine to run smoothly over curves and points; but in Stroudley's day maximum speeds rarely exceeded much over 60 m.p.h. Stroudley's constructional practice was the inspiration of many great engineers, notably the brothers Dugald and Peter Drummond, who between them carried their work to four Scottish and one English railway, while another disciple of Stroudley, A. W. Rendell, built many splendid locomotives for the East Indian Railway.

As the nineteenth century neared its end the need for more powerful locomotives on some overseas railways led to the development of the 4–6–0 type – always referred to as the 'Ten-wheeler' in the U.S.A. But first of all reference must be made to the inception and development of a remarkable Australian design which certainly ranks among the 'greats' of all time. Around the year 1890 the stature of Dugald Drummond, then on the Caledonian Railway, was immense, and when the Chief Commissioner of Railways in New South Wales sent his chief mechanical engineer, W. Thow, to the United Kingdom to discuss the supply of new locomotives it was to Drummond that he went. In October 1890, however, in Glasgow, Thow had apparently got little joy, and it was in consultation with the famous Manchester firm of Beyer, Peacock & Co., that he schemed out the design of a new 4–6–0. Just how much of it was derived from his discussions with Drummond it is not possible to say. But it was so much larger than anything that had gone before that at first grave doubts were expressed about the practicability of such a design. Arrived back in Sydney, however, Thow had no difficulty in securing authority for a first order for *fifty*, and this naturally went to Beyer, Peacock's. This was the truly great and famous 'P' class, the first of which took the road early in 1892. That, however, was not the end of it, splendid as was the subsequent career of the 'P' class engines in Australia. In Scotland, when the Highland Railway needed more powerful engines for its mountainous road over the Grampians, the New South Wales 'P' class design was copied with remarkable fidelity, and emerged as the first ever British 4–6–0. As such it is, of course, a famous design in its own right, and one of them is preserved in the Municipal Museum of Transport in Glasgow; but the true pioneer is 'Down Under', the joint work of Thow and Beyer, Peacock's.

In the new Highland engines there was a point of detail design that was of some significance towards the evolution of the locomotive. In the wild weather experienced in the north of Scotland difficulty sometimes ensued with exhaust steam beating down and obscuring the driver's outlook. David Jones the locomotive superintendent had devised a form of chimney having an outer ring, leaving an annular space between this and the true chimney; and by putting a series of louvres into the outer ring caused an upward draught of air to be induced in the annulus that carried the exhaust steam high and clear of the driver's lookout. In the U.S.A. in meeting the same problem, some designers adopted the unusual step of placing the driver's cab half-way along the boiler, leaving the fireman on his own on a platform at the rear of the firebox. The driver thus ensconced in a 'cupboard' by himself led to locomotives of this type being nicknamed 'Mother Hubbards'. For a time they were much favoured on railways in the eastern United States, including notably the Pennsylvania, and its associate the Atlantic City. The latter company at one time ran the fastest train in America between Philadelphia and Atlantic City.

In contrast to the increasing size, sophistication, and complexity of many new designs in America and on the continent of Europe during the last years of the nineteenth century the ultra-simple bogie four-coupled eight wheeler, the 4–4–0, was peculiarly and almost exclusively British; and when developed in the early years of the twentieth century by the addition of high-degree superheating, it attained on at least one English railway a standard of performance that few of the much larger and more complicated American and European contemporaries could equal, still less surpass. The simple British 4–4–0 was not the overnight brain child of some brilliant individual designer. It was a notable stage in a process of evolution in which good frame design, simple though superbly fabricated machinery, and a free-steaming boiler were embodied in a neat, gadget-free ensemble. The individual railways of Great Britain and Ireland developed styles which hallmarked them, without any need for distinguishing colours, or lettering – though to be sure the colourings were as beautiful as they were diverse. Some designers favoured outside cylinders, some outside frames; but the simplest and most popular form was with inside cylinders, and inside frames.

6

In the preceding paragraph I wrote that the 4–4–0 with inside cylinders and inside frames was peculiarly and almost exclusively British. Except that it was not so widely adopted, the 4–2–2 was even more so. British locomotive men cherished the 'single driver' as the express passenger type *par excellence*, and when developments of the historic Stephenson *Patentee* of the 2–2–2 type gave place to the 4–2–2 it seemed to some that perfection had indeed been attained. It is true that from a period roughly marked by the year 1870 the 'single' went into something of a decline. The increasing weight of trains made the superior adhesion of a four-coupled engine desirable, and the 2–4–0 began to supersede the 2–2–2; but then F. Holt, manager of the Midland Railway works at Derby, invented his steam sanding apparatus. This was partly the outcome of a rather fatuous dispute between the Midland Railway and the Westinghouse Brake Company, in which the latter objected to the use of the compressed-air plant installed on locomotives primarily for operating the brakes to be used also for applying sand to the rails, to improve adhesion in bad conditions. The Midland Railway was not to be dictated to by a contractor, and they not only developed the vacuum brake to the exclusion of the Westinghouse but also developed steam sanding. This was so successful that it led to the revival of the 'single' locomotive, not only in a series of magnificent 4–2–2s on the Midland itself but also in the further development of the type on the North Eastern, Great Central, Great Eastern, and Great Western, not to mention its continuance into the twentieth century on that railway where allegiance to it had scarcely wavered at all, the Great Northern.

How incredibly different was the developing railway situation in Southern Africa! There Cecil Rhodes' immortal dream of a 'Cape-to-Cairo Railway' was being doggedly pushed forward in conditions enough to daunt the most intrepid of explorers and colonisers. Through arid, inhospitable mountain terrain, over huge waterless deserts the line was driven northwards from the Cape towards the diamond fields of Kimberley and the fabulous gold deposits in the Transvaal. And when the Boer republics tended to be unco-operative to British developments Rhodes took another route west of this potentially hostile ground, northwards through Bechuanaland, into the country of the wild Matabele. This was to be the true Cape-to-

Cairo line, and it was carried on, through what is now Rhodesia, across the Zambesi River by the Victoria Falls and northwards towards the Congo. To save expense, and partly because of the extreme difficulties of the mountain country in the Cape, south of the Great Karroo desert, the rail gauge had been fixed at 3 ft. 6 in. High speed running, such as practised in Great Britain, France, and the U.S.A. was the last thing contemplated on the Cape-to-Cairo line, or anywhere else in Southern Africa. The maintenance of communication was all that mattered, and small lightly built locomotives that could climb steep gradients reliably with a fair load were the most suitable form of motive power. This was the day of the 4–8–0, many of which were eventually built for service in South Africa, Rhodesia, on the Uganda Railway, and elsewhere in the 'Dark Continent'.

Towards the end of the nineteenth century there were many attempts to improve the thermal efficiency of the steam locomotive. The ultra-simple British 4–4–0 was one of the cheapest and most reliable forms of railway motive power that had yet been devised; but its working efficiency in terms of work done in relation to the calorific value of the coal consumed was very low, and it depended also on supplies of the finest steam coal the world has ever known. Other countries were not so fortunate as Great Britain in the quality of their indigenous fuels, and there was every inducement for locomotive engineers to try and improve thermal efficiency. Presented with the success of two-stage and three-stage expansion of steam in marine engines, there was much experimenting with compound locomotives in the 1880s; but two-stage expansion in itself was no guarantee of greater efficiency in working. Theory and practice had to be skilfully blended in obtaining the ideal proportions for the volumes of the high-pressure and low-pressure cylinders, and much had to be learned about the absolute necessity of providing for free flow of steam between the high- and low-pressure systems. Few of the earlier compound locomotives were successful in these respects. It was the work of an Englishman, albeit one working in France, Alfred de Glehn, whose work on compound locomotives stood out above all others, and the range of 4-cylinder express passenger engines that he designed jointly with M. du Bousquet of the Northern Railway set new standards of train performance on the continent of Europe.

8

While the compound locomotives of Alfred de Glehn were making such a reputation in France a new era of locomotive practice in Great Britain was dawning. In the race from London to Aberdeen in August 1895 new world records for high-speed long-distance travel had been set up, and in the making of these the 4–4–0s of the Caledonian Railway had played a notable part. In general, these engines could be classed among the ultra-simple inside-cylinder designs traditional then of railways in Britain, but with an important difference: they had Dugald Drummond's very advanced design of cylinder and valve layout that made a better use of the steam than in most engines of the day. Consequently their boilers did not need to be unduly large. But the aftermath of the race, which had resulted in a 'win' for the West Coast companies, left an uneasy feeling that the competition might be renewed in the following summer, and the early spring of 1896 saw both sides building larger engines. On the Caledonian, the new locomotive superintendent, John F. McIntosh, took the very successful Drummond layout of cylinders and machinery and put on a much larger boiler. The results were astonishing. The new locomotives of the 'Dunalastair' class in working the tourist express between Carlisle and Perth in the late summer of 1896 were making times just as fast as those achieved in the height of the race in the previous summer, but with *double the loads*.

Details of this running were featured prominently in the technical press of the day, and created little short of a sensation – internationally. One result of this was that the Belgian State Railways asked John F. McIntosh to build some similar engines for them. This he could not do, but the directors of the Caledonian Railway were so pleased at the attention the 'Dunalastair' locomotives had created abroad that they permitted McIntosh to furnish drawings to the neighbouring firm of Neilson, Reid and Company, and to act as consultant while some of these engines were built under contract. In Europe, however, apart from Belgium and nearby Holland, compounds were 'all the go', and some ingenious, but rather complicated examples were built in Germany, for the Prussian State Railways. But the most important Continental development around the turn of the century was the application of the principle of superheated steam to locomotives by Dr. Wilhelm Schmidt, of Berlin. Hitherto the steam had been used, as boiled – to use a colloquialism

– its temperature corresponding to the pressure of formation. But already in stationary engine practice the advantage of heating the steam still further, after its formation, had been demonstrated. It became drier, more fluid, and its volume was much increased. The practice of 'superheating' brought many new problems, and the first Prussian locomotives embodying Schmidt's ideas were not entirely successful; but it was an important beginning. It was in England some ten years later that the full potentialities of the Schmidt superheater were to be demonstrated with such startling effect.

The Canadian Pacific Railway, in its vast extent and in the diversity of physical conditions and operating needs in different localities, provided great problems to those responsible for motive power. Until the 1920s it was indeed the only single administration whose tracks extended across the entire width of the North American Continent, from coast to coast, and in latitudes where the width was greatest. In that extraordinary span the locomotive department had to provide for long hauls at medium speed across the prairies, for exceptional haulage effort on the tremendous inclines in the Rockies, and the Selkirks, and for fast highly competitive inter-city services between Montreal, Ottawa, and Toronto. In the Maritime provinces competition was no less keen. In its early years, and for some time after, however, the C.P.R. pursued a motive-power policy not unlike that of thirty years later on the L.M.S. in England, in building up a large stud of general-purpose locomotives of moderate power, and using them in multiple where greater power was needed. As on the L.M.S. also the chosen type was the 4–6–0 of gradually increasing size up to the splendid 'D 10'. On the original alignment of the Field Hill, British Columbia, the gradient was 1 in 25, and one 4–6–0 was capable of taking no more than two of the standard cars. At that time few trains required less than three locomotives and they were spaced at intervals. A common formation was: locomotive, two cars, locomotive, four cars, locomotive. It was only on the eastern lines that special-purpose fast-speed locomotives were used.

The Austrian State Railways – the 'Imperial Royal Austrian State Railways', to give them their full title – included many sections of severe mountain climbing, and they had as locomotive superintendent a very distinguished engineer in Herr Karl Gölsdorf. One of the difficulties experienced by most designers of compound locomotives was to devise a simple method of starting, because in the ordinary way the low-pressure cylinders could not exert any torque until steam had first passed through the high-pressure system. Many different starting valves were invented, usually relying on skilled manipulation by the driver; but Gölsdorf designed an arrangement that operated automatically, and was thus simple to work. His earlier compounds had only two cylinders, like those of the Prussian engineer Von Borries. The cylinders were outside, and to see such a locomotive from the front was extraordinary because the two cylinders were of different sizes. He built quite a variety of these engines, for different duties, because in addition to mountain climbing on the Arlberg route through the Tyrol the main line of the State railway included many fast-running stretches, particularly between Salzburg and Vienna. The 2–8–0 locomotives designed specially for the Arlberg route were very successful, and some of them put in more than seventy years service. How Herr Gölsdorf developed his system of compounding to use four cylinders, with even greater success, is told later.

For upwards of a hundred years provision of motive power for the Indian railways had been a major task for the British locomotive building industry. Quite apart from technicalities, the administrative conditions were unusual, not in the differences existing between the various railways but in there being varying degrees of 'half-way house' between full state ownership and the freedom and independence enjoyed by the old railway companies of Great Britain. Within these limitations, and always bearing in mind that ultimately all the Indian railways would become fully state-owned, there was much of the pride in company, and the cherishing of individual practices that characterised the old railways of Great Britain. Nevertheless, by the turn of the century, mindful of future evolution that seemed inevitable, irrespective of any political changes between India and Great Britain, the fact of operating conditions being similar over a large proportion of the Indian broad-gauge mileage made the opportunities for standardisation of locomotives seem favourable. In the early years of the twentieth century the British Engineering Standards Association (BESA), in collaboration with the consulting engineers to the Indian Government, prepared a series of standard designs that from the viewpoint of route availability were widely accepted. They included an Indian version of the two most popular and traditional British designs – 4–4–0 for passenger and 0–6–0 for goods. Many of the latter are still in service in India today.

The success achieved by the de Glehn compound system – with two high-pressure cylinders outside, and two low-pressure cylinders inside, and the drive divided between the two coupled axles – on the Northern Railway of France in three successively enlarged versions of the original 4–4–0 design was such that when the increasing weight of express trains and the need for higher average speeds called for the design to be enlarged the 'Atlantic' was chosen, in order to provide a much larger boiler and firebox. Two remarkable engines, Nos 2641 and 2642, were built in 1900, at de Glehn's works, the Société Alsacienne de Constructions Méchaniques, in Belfort, and they were put to work on the English boat trains between Paris and Calais. Here they came under the scrutiny of the distinguished author of international fame, Charles Rous-Marten. In the most eulogistic vein he wrote of their prowess, and due in no small measure to this publicity, the design was taken up by a number of different railways. One of these engines, the *La France*, was purchased by the Great Western Railway of England; a small batch was built for the Egyptian State Railways to run the De Luxe tourist expresses between Cairo and Luxor, and in later years the Bengal Nagpur Railway adopted a larger version as their standard express passenger type. But the finest of these derivatives from the Nord 'Atlantics', and perhaps least known outside their own country, were those of no more than slightly larger basic proportions on the Paris–Orleans Railway, of which design two further examples were imported by the Great Western Railway in 1905, and named *President* and *Alliance*.

In Imperial Germany in the last dozen or so years before the First World War the railway situation was administratively rather complex. Following the Franco-Prussian war of 1870–71 and the annexation of much territory from France, the German chancellor, Bismarck attempted to bring all railways in the newly consolidated empire under a unified state control. But this proposal met with such opposition from the states in the south that it was dropped for a time, and not renewed until after the First World War when Germany had become a republic. So, although the influence of Prussia was strong, the state railway systems of Saxony, Baden, and Bavaria, to name only three, went their own way in locomotive development. Compounds were still generally favoured, particularly in Bavaria, where the firm of Maffei, in Munich, had a notable record of successful designs. In Prussia itself, however, the work of Dr. Schmidt in developing the superheater convinced many engineers, not only in Germany, that considerable improvements in thermal efficiency theoretically possible with compound expansion could be more simply and reliably attained by the use of superheated steam; and although the Prussian State Railways continued to add compound locomotives to their large stock, there was introduced the very successful 2-cylinder simple 4–6–0 of class 'P8' in 1906, which was destined to become not only one of the most numerically strong of all German steam locomotive classes but also to be one of the very few of the old State system designs to be accepted as a national standard after the unification of the railways in 1920.

With the Battle of the Gauges in England so convincingly decided against Brunel and the 7 ft. gauge on the Great Western there seemed to be universal agreement on the need for a unified system – for a time at any rate. In India particularly, when the Marquis of Dalhousie, as Governor General, was laying down the principles on which the railway network of the country should be built he was emphatic that whatever rail gauge was decided upon should be adopted everywhere. In Great Britain, however, the remarkable success of Robert Fairlie's small steam locomotives on the 1 ft. 11½ in. gauge Festiniog Railway in North Wales rather went to his head, and he opened a positive crusade in favour of narrow-gauge lines, arguing that they could be built with cheapness and operated with economy, whereas the broad gauge could be run only with extravagance. He wrote a full length book entitled *The Battle of the Gauges Renewed*. While it was never likely that his self-confident eloquence would disturb the established networks in Great Britain, on the continent of Europe and in America it was a time when many new railways were being projected for colonising purposes, or for serving areas of pioneer industrial activity. In these Fairlie saw his opportunity. Even before then, however, the situation in India had developed to the extent that a network of metre-gauge feeder lines to the main broad-gauge system had been authorised, and this principle was carried still further by the building of still narrower-gauge railways in remote areas. Of these there is no more picturesque or spectacular example than the Darjeeling Himalaya Railway.

Herr Karl Gölsdorf was one of the most progressive of all European locomotive engineers of the early 1900s. He was strongly international in his interest and friendships, and on his visits to Great Britain he became deeply impressed with the beauty of line evident in so many British locomotives. His own designs, up to the turn of the century, had been starkly functional, though not perhaps to the same extent as some of those on the neighbouring railways of Hungary. But in the early 1900s a profound change began to come over the new locomotive designs he introduced on the Austrian State Railways, and from designs that, to take the most charitable view of them, were anything but 'easy on the eye' he advanced to some of the most elegant and beautifully finished locomotives ever to run on the continent of Europe. In this transition also he developed his compound system from two to four cylinders. This of course provided a better-balanced machine for a fast-running express locomotive, but he applied it also on designs intended for heavy gradient and fast freight work. So far as boiler design was concerned he could not, of course, follow British practice because in locomotives of greater power he needed large fireboxes to burn the indigenous coal. It was this consideration that led to his adoption of the 2–6–4 rather than the 4–6–2 type for maximum passenger duties.

French interest in the de Glehn system of compounding became increasingly widespread in the early 1900s, though not everywhere in the same physical form as on the Northern Railway. Early experience on the Eastern Railway was a little mixed. Some 4–cylinder compound 4–4–0s of larger size than any of the Nord varieties were introduced, and by some freak of operation that was never entirely explained, these engines were addicted to slipping, differentially between the forward and after pair of coupled wheels, and this led to buckling of the coupling rods. As a temporary expedient these latter were removed, putting the engines into the form once familiar in England on the 3-cylinder Webb compounds of the London and North Western Railway, with the high- and low-pressure cylinders driving separate and uncoupled axles. This feature was included on the very first de Glehn compound 4–4–0 on the Nord, but was not repeated. Whereas the latter railway progressed from the 4–4–0 to the 'Atlantic' when larger locomotives were required, it was perhaps significant in view of their early troubles with adhesion that the Eastern adopted the 4–6–0 type. Whatever the shortcomings of the compound 4–4–0s may have been, the 4-cylinder compound 4–6–0 was one of the really great French designs of the period, and had a long and distinguished record of excellent service.

While over much of Continental Europe the compound locomotive was much in vogue in the 1900–14 period, it was not adopted in Holland. This was not entirely due to British manufacturing influence, strong though it remained, because some of the smaller independent railways were inclined to 'go shopping' for locomotives in Germany. But over much of Holland there was a major problem, not so acutely experienced elsewhere, when it came to introducing larger and more powerful locomotives. The ground was soft and not ideal for heavy load bearing, and the civil engineers had been forced to impose severe restrictions upon the axle-loads of locomotives. The State railway had developed the classic Beyer-Peacock 4–4–0 into an inside-cylindered Atlantic type for the mail trains operated from Flushing; but this, with its limited adhesion weight, was not a suitable type for general introduction. It was nevertheless realised that axle loading alone is not the only factor in the working of a locomotive that affects the track and under-line bridges. There is the 'dynamic augment' effect of the balance weights used to ensure smooth running, and on a two-cylinder simple engine the effect of these, at a speed of 60 m.p.h., can increase the loading on the track to some 50 per cent more than the dead weight carried on the axles. The Dutch civil and mechanical engineers in consultation determined that if instead of two cylinders four were used, and all driving on the same axle, the dynamic augment was eliminated, and a heavier basic axle load could be accepted. This was the basis of the important and very successful 4-cylinder simple 4–6–0 introduced in 1910.

On the massively built, and well-ballasted main lines of Great Britain axle loading had not yet become an urgent consideration in the early 1900s, nor was the effect of the dynamic augment, or 'hammer blow' as it was commonly called, fully appreciated. The ultra-simple inside cylinder 4–4–0, so popular on the British railways, was actually one of the worst offenders in this respect, but it was not until the setting up of a Bridge Stress Committee in the early 1920s that its effect showed quantitatively. In the meantime the inside cylinder 4–4–0 with the valuable addition of superheating, as propounded by Dr. Wilhelm Schmidt, was rising to its greatest heights of achievement. There was nevertheless considerable divergence of opinion as to how best to use these advantages. Some engineers took it as an opportunity to use lower boiler pressures, and thus reduce maintenance costs; others used no more than a moderate degree of superheat, to avoid throwing away any unused heat energy in the exhaust steam. But on the London and North Western Railway C. J. Bowen Cooke used the same steam pressure as previously, and a high degree of superheat, and produced a locomotive of phenomenal capacity, for its size and weight, in his 'George the Fifth' class of 1910.

Had it not been for the rather insular outlook of many railway administrations of the day, and a situation in which many students of mechanical engineering practice and locomotion did not cast their nets particularly wide, it would have become apparent that the ordinary day-to-day work of the 'George the Fifth' class locomotives between London, Liverpool, and Manchester, and between Crewe and Carlisle, was the equal, if not the superior, of practically any performance then being made by the considerably larger locomotives on the continent of Europe. In the detailed reference to the design accompanying the picture of the *Coronation* engine of 1911 it is explained how these astonishing engines rather overtaxed their strength in the process. But the facts of performance speak for themselves.

In contrast to the type of service in which these LNWR 4–4–0 locomotives made their name, the mountain railways of Switzerland posed some interesting problems for the locomotive engineer, particularly on certain lines that included a mixture of normal and exceedingly steep mountain gradients that required rack rails. It would have been inconvenient to stop at the beginning and end of such sections to change from normal to rack locomotives, and in 1905 an ingenious design was produced by the Swiss Locomotive Works, of Winterthur, that could be used in both types of conditions. The first locomotives of this type were 0–6–0 tank engines for the Brünig Railway in Switzerland. They were 4-cylinder compounds but worked compound only on the rack sections. The high-pressure cylinders drive the road wheels, while the low-pressure cylinders, when operable, drive the rack pinions.

So far as European compounds go, the collaboration between Maffei and Bavarian State Railways must be considered almost as successful as that in the early 1900s between de Glehn and the Northern Railway of France. In the former case it reached its pinnacle in the production of the famous Class S 3/6 4-cylinder compound Pacifics in 1908. They may not be everyone's idea of a handsome locomotive, having many angular and functional features, and the chimney appears too tall for the rest of the boiler mountings. But as will be appreciated from the detailed description of the design accompanying the beautiful Meadway painting the mechanical conception was very sound and effective.

In Belgium, after the period of extreme neatness in locomotive design that followed the importing of the five 'Dunalastairs' from Scotland, there began a time of extraordinary development. The fame of the de Glehn 4-cylinder compounds in France had its inevitable effect in Belgium, and as early as 1905 a batch of 4–6–0s was put into service. The earlier ones were non-superheated, but such was their success that a further seventy-five, with superheaters were ordered after the First World War. With various modifications and rebuildings no fewer than sixty-nine of them survived the *Second* World War. Despite their success, and the perpetuation of the design for so long, the de Glehn compound system was not retained when it came to building still larger engines, and in 1910 Monsieur J. B. Flamme designed the first Belgian 'Pacifics'. They were 4-cylinder simples, and could well be set down as one of the most mis-shapen locomotives ever built. To enable the inside cylinders to drive the leading coupled axle they had to be set well forward, beneath a long open platform in front of the boiler. It was perhaps not surprising that so revolutionary a design was not an immediate success; but as told in the notes accompanying the Meadway painting, they were subjected to various modifications and eventually became very fine and reliable locomotives – if not exactly handsome.

The 4–6–0 type is one that is not generally associated with the railways of the U.S.A., largely because of the glamour attached to the 'Pacifics' and still larger engines that followed them; but actually the 4–6–0 was a very useful, popular, and widely used type, for

17

general service, and records show that at one time no fewer than 17,000 of them were at work, or no more than recently retired. Most of them were of the mixed traffic type, with coupled wheels of about 5 ft. 9 in. diameter. Indeed, the Pennsylvania built a series, new, in their Altoona shops as recently as 1935. At the turn of the century, however, the 4–6–0 was also used for express passenger work, though it was not generally favoured. Presence of the large diameter driving wheels at the rear end made it necessary to use a narrow firebox in which the class of coal normally available for locomotive purposes in the U.S.A. was not burned to the best advantage. In this gallery of fame an express passenger 4–6–0 has been chosen to represent the U.S.A., partly because of the interesting comparison it affords with engines of the same wheel arrangement in other parts of the world, but equally because it was an excellent locomotive in itself.

A difficult terrain and the handicap of the 3 ft. 6 in. gauge did nothing to quench the enterprise of the New Zealand Railways. Locomotive design had many interesting features, and unlike sub-standard gauge lines in many other parts of the world, there was no hesitation about running fast. Speeds of 60 m.p.h. if not required by the ordinary schedules were not infrequently attained when making up time. Whereas all the earlier influences in Australia were British, locomotive practice in New Zealand was derived more from a study of American methods, with a dash of French thrown in, and this was particularly the case with the 'Ab' class of Pacific engine, first introduced in 1915. It has been truly said that this class of loco-motive was virtually synonymous with the development of the New Zealand Railways for a full forty years after its first introduction. Although there had been trials of compounding, the 'Ab' was a simple, straightforward 2-cylinder machine, with outside Wals-chaerts valve gear, and a skilfully designed chassis that provided safe and comfortable riding at maximum speed, and so encouraged drivers to run hard when occasion demanded it.

The New Zealand 'Ab' was one of those great locomotive designs that habitually put up work that would be considered beyond its theoretical capacity. It had a counterpart, though one of a very different type, in England, on the Great Northern Railway. When H. A. Ivatt succeeded Patrick Stirling as locomotive superintendent in 1896 he largely reversed his predecessor's policy by building engines with boilers that were exceptionally large for the period. Though tremendously impressive in appearance, the cylinders were so small that no more than a moderate tractive power could at first be realised. Again, when superheating was first applied Ivatt reduced the boiler pressure, so making the later engines no more powerful than the earlier ones. At that time, around 1910, it was not of any great consequence, for Great Northern timetables did not demand very fast running with the heavier trains. But the changes subsequently wrought by H. N. Gresley, in applying a very high degree of superheat, in conjunction with well-designed piston valves fairly transformed the engines; and unless one was there to observe it personally, some of the work performed in the 1930s was almost unbelievable. No locomotives deserved the description 'great' more than the high superheat 'Atlantics' of the former Great Northern Railway.

The story of competitive railway building across Canada in the early years of the present century is at the same time a romance and a tragedy, in that intransigence and over-optimism led to the concurrent building of not one but two closely contiguous and fiercely competitive lines from Winnipeg to the west. It was generally agreed that after the outstanding success of the Canadian Pacific a second line was needed; but two could mean financial suicide for both, and so it very nearly proved. Had not war come in 1914 and the need for keeping both the new competitors in operation, it is probable that both the Canadian Northern and the Grand Trunk Pacific would have gone completely bankrupt. As it was, they were kept going by Government assistance. Both had been finely equipped, and the 4–6–0 of the Canadian Northern, which is the subject of the Meadway painting, is one of a large class that had a long and successful career. It was in some ways the counterpart of the Canadian 'Pacific' 'D 10' 4–6–0.

The 4–6–0 type was much commoner, and much more popular, in Canada than in the U.S.A. while in Great Britain it can be regarded as the most popular wheel arrangement of all time. Some years ago a discussion took place as to what was the most representative British passenger locomotive – if one had to select a design to stand for the country as a whole; and the choice, from simplicity and symmetry of outline, wheel arrangement, style of painting and general *décor* fell upon the 'King Arthur' class of the Southern Railway. This famous class, like the Great Northern 'Atlantic' mentioned earlier, belongs to that group of designs that in its earliest form did not come fully up to expectations, whereas, a few expert touches, highly significant in themselves but doing very little to alter the external appearance, transformed the engines into a really brilliant design. In the case of the Southern 'King Arthurs', the change from the original London and South Western 'N 15' class was mainly in respect of the draughting arrangements in the smoke-box, which vastly improved the steaming.

At a time when the whole trend of current British locomotive practice was towards 3- or 4-cylinder designs, and the Southern itself was producing the larger and more powerful 4-cylinder 4–6–0s of the 'Lord Nelson' class, the 'King Arthur' was considered by some to be a little old-fashioned – not 'with it', as the colloquialism goes. But actually the 'King Arthur', and the L. & S.W.R. 'N 15' from which it was developed represented the shape of things to come – if not immediately in Great Britain, then certainly in the U.S.A. In 1911 the Pennsylvania, in many ways the 'Premier Line' of North America, settled finally for the 2-cylinder simple, with outside Walschaerts valve gear in the large 'K 2' class Pacific, and followed this in 1915 by what was then considered the enormous superheated 'K 4' 'Pacific', with a tractive effort nearly double that of all but a very few British locomotives of the day.

The success of the 'K 4' verily turned the tide against the compound in the U.S.A., except in one particular area. The American railways had in a big way taken up the precepts of Anatole Mallet in applying the compound principle to two entirely separate engine units beneath one large boiler, with the leading unit – usually the low pressure – articulated, so that the very long engine wheelbase could negotiate curves easily. The articulated compound Mallet was developed to tremendous sizes in the U.S.A., for heavy freight work on severe gradients; but it was essentially a slow-running machine. At any appreciable speed, with the normal form of suspension, it was not very stable, and because of the long interconnection pipes between the two engine units there were considerable heat and pressure losses that hindered performance at anything but the slowest uphill speeds.

While the years of the First World War and the early 1920s saw the American railways in general turning to the 2-cylinder simple locomotive, and the British, following the findings of the Bridge Stress Committee, settling more and more towards 3- and 4-cylinder simples, the French, without exception, remained faithful to the 4-cylinder compound. During the war the 'Pacific' design of the État system had been purchased in quantity, both from such French firms as were able to continue with locomotive manufacture and also from the North British Locomotive Company in Glasgow. The Government, hoping for general standardisation, urged upon all the railways the desirability of accepting this type for future use; but both the Nord and the Paris, Lyons and Mediterranean had strongly held traditions in locomotive practice, and both successfully resisted this attempt to impose the État design of Pacific upon them. The Nord under the direction of M. Bréville brought out a magnificent new 'Super-Pacific' design, the work of which on the English boat trains was soon attracting world-wide attention.

In the meantime British development in multi-cylindered single expansion reached a new climax in 1927 with the production of the Great Western Railway 'King' class, having for an engine weight of no more than 89 tons the exceptional tractive effort of 40,300 lb. It was the culmination of the development of the 4-cylinder 4–6–0 express passenger locomotive begun by G. J. Churchward, at Swindon, after his experience with the de Glehn compound 'Atlantics' purchased from France in 1903 and 1905. The details of these remarkable locomotives are discussed more fully alongside the painting of the pioneer engine of this new class; but it must be emphasised that much of their success was due to the availability of very high-grade steam coal, and in a form that enabled it to be fired to the very best advantage.

I have written earlier of the developments of railways in Southern Africa, and the absence of any need for high speeds on the 3 ft. 6 in. trunk lines northward from the Cape. As matters developed after the First World War there was considerable speeding up, concurrently with the improvement of the track. Although hindered by the 3 ft. 6 in. gauge, the South African Railways had no loading gauge restrictions to constrain the upward and outward increase in locomotive dimensions, beyond that of running stability, and by the

1930s some truly mammoth engines were in operation. These were uniformly of the 2-cylinder simple type, with outside valve gear; and while extensive trial and regular use was made of certain poppet valve gears, the most successful in the long run was the well-tried Walschaerts radial gear actuating large-diameter piston valves.

In the Empire of India the process of standardisation of locomotive design continued during the later 1920s, though despite the advantage, to the engine designer, of the extra width between the frames of the 5 ft. 6 in. gauge, and despite the continuing strong British influence, the large new standard types were uniformly 2-cylinder simples, with outside Walschaerts valve'gear. For passenger work there were three classes of 'Pacific' designated 'XA', 'XB', and 'XC' in ascending order of duties, the first being the light branch class and the 'XC' the heavy express passenger, used on the mail trains and other maximum tasks of railways like the North Western and the East Indian. The corresponding freight types were the 'XD' and 'XE', heavy 2-8-2s. They were all handsomely proportioned, massively built engines, essentially British in appearance, and many of them have put in more than forty years of hard service.

It was perhaps inevitable that some of the Indian railways, following their old traditions of independence, should have obtained authority to order variations of these standard designs. The North Western had a 4-cylinder variant of the 'XC' Pacific, while the Great Indian Peninsula had two experimental 4-6-2s generally similar to the 'XB' class but with Caprotti valve gear, roller bearings throughout, and thermic siphons in the firebox. Then, throughout the period between the two world wars the Bengal Nagpur Railway, remaining completely independent, pursued its own locomotive policy. Following its earlier use of de Glehn compound 'Atlantics', this railway took delivery from the North British Locomotive Company in 1928 of some magnificent 4-cylinder de Glehn compound 'Pacifics', which were among the most distinctive and outstanding locomotives on the railways of British India. The practice of the Northern Railway of France had been studied closely at the time these engines were designed, and an interesting feature of the Bréville Super-Pacifics' incorporated was the use of balanced slide valves for the low-pressure cylinders.

In France itself by the year 1930 the centre of interest was passing to the Paris–Orleans Railway. Train loads were much on the increase. The electrified system had been extended southwards to Tours on the main line to Bordeaux, and to Vierzon on that to Toulouse, and some augmentation of steam locomotive capacity was needed to avoid any disparity in running standards north and south of the stations where there was a change in traction. Mention has already been made of the really splendid de Glehn compound 'Atlantics' introduced in the early 1900s. The 'Pacifics' that followed them – the first of the 4–6–2 type ever to run in Europe – had been something of a disappointment, with their actual performance falling considerably short of the levels one would have expected from a comparison of their proportions with those of the 'Atlantics'. It is true that the latter were exceptionally good, but what had been achieved with the earlier engines ought at least to have been possible with the larger ones, and what proved to be a classic research was set in train to find out what was wrong. The result of the work of a young engineer named André Chapelon was the rebuilding of engine No. 3566, to provide some phenomenal results and establish entirely new standards of French – and world! – locomotive performance.

In writing of the new standard locomotives in India during the 1920s I referred to the advantages of the 5 ft. 6 in. gauge to the engine designer. One country where hitherto no advantage had been taken of this facility was South Australia, having the 5 ft. 3 in. gauge. It is to be feared that the Government had taken a rather parsimonious attitude towards railway development until the year 1922, when a new Railway Commissioner was appointed. The route of the Interstate expresses between Adelaide and Melbourne certainly had some hard climbing to do in the Mount Lofty ranges; but the largest engines then available were elderly 4–6–0s capable of hauling no more than 190 tons unassisted. The new commissioner said he wanted engines that would haul at least *double* that load. Fortunately the reigning chief mechanical engineer, who averred that the thing could not be done, was due for retirement, and Commissioner Webb waited his time, and then renewed his demands upon the successor, F. J. Shea. The outcome was a range of colossal and outstanding locomotives, all built in England, by Sir W. G. Armstrong-Whitworth and Co. of Newcastle-upon-Tyne.

Equally 'great', both in conception and size, was a class of twenty-four general-purpose 4–8–4s built in 1934–35 for the Chinese National Railways by the Vulcan Foundry. Locomotives of maximum power and versatility were needed, to cope with the steeply graded northern section of the Canton-Hankow line, and also to make relatively fast time over the level stretches of the Shanghai–Nanking Railway. A major consideration, however, was the development of maximum power in all circumstances on low-grade coal. The mechanical engineering adviser to the Chinese Government at that time was a British engineer of very wide experience, K. Cantlie, who had been trained on the London and North Western Railway, at Crewe, as a premium pupil of C. J. Bowen Cooke, and had subsequently had appointments in South America and India. Under his guidance the specification of what proved an outstanding locomotive was drawn up. It was immediately successful when new, but has subsequently withstood all the varying and hazardous conditions that have prevailed in China. The latest information is that some of these great engines are still in use, forty years after their first introduction.

The main line of the New York Central system, between New York and Chicago, was for the most part level throughout, so much so that it was able to maintain equality of overall running time with the Pennsylvania between the two cities, although its distance of 960 miles was nearly 50 miles longer. The Pennsylvania cut through the heart of the Allegheny mountains and had some difficult gradients and severe curvature in consequence. It was in 1927 that the NYC received its first 4–6–4, or 'Hudson' type express locomotive, the advantage over the previous 'Pacifics' being to accommodate a larger firebox and give greater sustained horsepower at high speed. This was necessary to maintain a high average speed with heavy loads on level track. And they *were* heavy loads on the NYC. Unless an express train scaled more than 1,000 tons, it was hardly worth pulling – or so it seemed to an onlooker. From the J-Ia of 1927 the design was developed over the years up to the J-3a of 1937, by the end of which latter year there were 245 'Hudsons' in service. These included those allocated to railroads associated with the NYC, namely the Michigan Central, the Boston and Albany, and 'Big Four' (Chicago, Cleveland, Cincinatti, and St. Louis). Finally, there was a batch of ten built in 1938 with a streamlined exterior, and allocated to trains like the 'Twentieth Century Limited', and the 'Empire State Express'. But the 'J-3a', no less than its predecessors from 'J-1a' onwards, was a truly 'great' locomotive, whether it had a streamlined covering on it or not.

Streamlining on steam locomotives is sometimes dismissed as a 'gimmick'; an eye-catching publicity ruse that has no practical view, and can be, in fact, detrimental rather than useful because of the closing in of much of the working machinery. The first major British instance of streamlining was in quite a different category. On the London and North Eastern Railway considerable trouble had been experienced on the large 2–8–2 engines of the 'Cock o' the North' class with exhaust steam clinging to the top of the boiler and beating down to obscure the driver's lookout. One way to cure this trouble was to add side deflector plates, sometimes termed 'blinkers', but Gresley disliked these, on aesthetic grounds, and when the time came to build the special 'Pacific' engines for the high-speed 'Silver Jubilee' express in 1935, that were to be streamlined for publicity purposes, he adopted the form of front-end fairing used on the high-speed Bugatti railcars recently introduced in France. This was not true aerodynamic screening, but a wedge shape, and it proved extremely successful in throwing the exhaust steam upwards and clear of the cab. Tests in a wind tunnel showed that the stream-lined form saved a little power at high speed, but the *real* bonus was the solution of the smoke nuisance. It was the changes in the mechanical design, as described alongside the painting of the engine *Silver Fox*, that made the new engines so extremely free running and so economical.

Towards the end of the 1930s the streamlined age on railways had arrived in full measure, and in the U.S.A. several railroads retaining steam as their premier form of first-line motive power built locomotives of startling appearance to run their prestige express trains. In days before the development of civil aviation there was extremely keen competition for traffic between major cities, and perhaps nowhere quite so thrusting as between Chicago and Milwaukee, where the Chicago and North Western and the Chicago, Milwaukee, St. Paul and Pacific were hot rivals. In 1939 the eastbound morning 'Hiawatha' express was booked to cover the 410½ miles from St.

25

Paul to Chicago in 390 minutes, including seven stops totalling 19 minutes standing intermediately, with the final 85 miles from Milwaukee covered in 75 minutes start-to-stop. When these trains were first on, with a limited load of only six cars, some special streamlined 'Atlantic' locomotives were built specially for the job. But the high-speed runs proved so popular that heavier formations became necessary, and in 1938 some remarkable 4–6–4 locomotives were introduced capable of taking an increased regular load of nine cars, and of dealing with augmented loads of up to *fifteen* on the same schedules, which involved regular running at 100 m.p.h. on level track.

The 4–6–4 type came to be regarded as the North American standard for heavy high-speed work on level or easy gradients, leaving the 4–8–2 and the 4–8–4 for the more heavily graded routes. In Canada the 4–6–4 was the standard passenger type on all sections of the CPR other than over the exceptionally difficult mountain divisions between Calgary and Revelstoke. The ultimate development of the 4–6–4 on the Canadian Pacific took place in 1937, when what has been described as a semi-streamlined style was applied. But the lines of these new engines were simplified by comparison with those of their predecessors by the adoption of a domeless boiler. This class achieved its lasting distinction at the time of the Royal Tour of Canada in 1939 when one of these engines, selected to haul the Royal Train, was given an exhibition finish in royal blue and aluminium, with a crown at the front end of each running board. After the visit the engine concerned, No. 2850, had the standard CPR livery, but with the consent of His Majesty, King George VI, the name 'Royal Hudson' was given to the entire class of forty-five locomotives, and all had the distinctive crowns added to the front end of the running plate. Several of these engines have been preserved, and while two are purely museum pieces, a third is in active service on the British Columbia Railway, working special trips on the highly scenic line between North Vancouver and Squamish.

The distinction as to what constitutes a 'great' locomotive may be open to debate, and nothing could be more truly Irish than some sort of argument! So my choice of a locomotive design of which only three examples were built could well be a matter of controversy. But Edgar Bredin's 3-cylinder 4–6–0s named after the ancient Irish

queens were not only much the largest and most powerful locomotives ever to run in Ireland but they were also some of the most
beautiful, in addition to being superb machines in traffic. I realise
that in writing in such superlatives I am laying myself open to
argument, if not outright criticism; because the work of the three
great Queens has not been as fully documented by a long way as
some of the locomotives of the Great Northern Railway, or even
of the Northern Counties Committee section of the LMSR. But
I had the privilege of seeing *Maeve*, the first of the three Queens, in
action, of riding her during a particular tough assignment, and if my
opinion of her merits brings me a metaphorical crack over the head
from the shillelagh of a rival partisan I am prepared to risk it.
Seriously though, *Maeve* and her two sisters were splendid examples
of locomotive practice, and a fit culmination of the long and distin-
quished record of construction at Inchicore Works, Dublin.

I have told earlier how it was once thought that the coupling of
driving wheels was a hindrance to the free-running of a locomotive,
and how in England designers reverted to the 4–2–2 type as soon as
the steam sanding gear was invented, and reliable adhesion obtained
with a single pair of driving wheels. Something near the complete
negation of such a theory was obtained in the many varieties of
eight-coupled locomotive in use in North America in the 1930s,
while even in Great Britain we had the Gresley 'Cock o' the North'
2–8–2s on the LNER, which could attain 85 m.p.h. with ease. But
perhaps the most remarkable instance of an eight-coupled design
combining the attributes of a mighty hill-climber with an ability to
run at 100 m.p.h. on straight, favourable stretches was to be seen on
the Atchison, Topeka and Santa Fé Railroad in the U.S.A. There,
huge 4–8–4s, oil-fired, used to run trains of more than 1,000 tons
trailing load, throughout over the 1,234 miles from La Junta,
Colorado, to Los Angeles, and on the longer route from Kansas City
via Belen, New Mexico, to Los Angeles, a total of 1,788 miles in one
continuous assignment. The first Santa Fé 4–8–4s went into service
in 1927, and the culmination of a very successful development
came in 1938, with the class of locomotive shown in the Meadway
painting.

These great engines put in some tremendous work on the heavily
augmented express trains to the west coast during the Second World

27

War, when it was urgently necessary for high-ranking service personnel and business men to get through to the strategic bases quickly. It was war service of a kind very different from that required in Europe, where speed became a secondary consideration and the reliable haulage of munitions and supplies was the main criterion. Equally the need was for locomotives that would run with an absolute minimum of maintenance, both in terms of daily attention and of visits to main works for general overhaul. Furthermore, as the war progressed there arose an urgent need to avoid the use of the more sophisticated materials in locomotive construction. High-grade alloy steels and such like were needed for aircraft and other weapons. Locomotives had to be built with the simplest of materials. These principles were carried further than anywhere else in the German 'Kriegslokomotiv' – an austerity version of a successful pre-war 2–10–0, which was built in the thousands, for general service in all the countries under German military occupation as well as in Germany itself. In the elimination of all refinements of design and reduction to the barest stark necessities, it was a remarkable example of locomotive construction.

In some respects the period of rehabilitation after the war imposed problems more difficult than some of those experienced in the war itself. This was especially the case in France. Before and during the period of re-entry of allied forces on to the continent of Europe systematic bombing of railway targets was incessant, and enormous damage was done to junctions, locomotive depots, bridges, and workshops to cause the maximum hindrance to movement in the rear of the enemy's battle line. In consequence, as France became liberated there was a desperate shortage of railway equipment that was serviceable, when it became urgently necessary to re-open the lines that had been breached. So far as locomotives were concerned this situation had been foreseen even before the end of the war, and in 1944 a French mission had visited the U.S.A. to arrange for bulk supplies of new locomotives. With the ready co-operation of the Baldwin Locomotive Works, Philadelphia, a design of 2–8–2 general-service locomotive was worked out – the celebrated '141 R' – and orders for no fewer than 1,340 were given to firms in the U.S.A. and Canada.

In India the motive-power situation had become critical before even the war had spread to South East Asia. The general recession that had affected the entire world during the 1930s had been particularly serious in India, and the natural outcome had been a slowing down in the replacement of obsolescent stock on the railways. Furthermore, the standard designs of 'Pacific' locomotives, in continuous heavy use, had shown certain shortcomings. A new design was worked out, but it was not until 1942 that first orders were placed with the Baldwin Locomotive Works for engines of the new 'WP' class – a simple, straightforward 2-cylinder 'Pacific' embodying the experience of many years operating with the existing 'XB' and 'XC' Pacifics. The design was wholly Indian, the decision to incorporate a degree of streamlining, though perhaps a questionable adornment in war-time, imparted a degree of individuality to a new class, and one that has subsequently been exploited to pleasing effect on the Regional systems in the India of today.

A main line of exceptional difficulty that was called upon to play a vital part of the allied war effort was that of the Canadian Pacific eastward through the mountain ranges of British Columbia and into Alberta. The day had fortunately long passed when the Field Hill had a gradient of 1 in 25. The construction of the two spectacular spiral tunnels had reduced the maximum inclination to 1 in 45; but the operation of heavy passenger trains of more than 1,000 tons trailing load, and still more so of enormous freight trains, provided great problems, not least in the conditions experienced by the crews of hard-worked locomotives in the confined single-tracked bores of the spiral tunnels. Conditions generally were no easier in the passage farther west through the Selkirk Range, westbound up the notorious Beaver Hill, and eastbound on the climb from Revelstoke through the dreaded Laurie Tunnel. Even though huge oil-fired locomotives of the 2–10–4 or 'Selkirk' type had been introduced, double-, and sometimes triple-heading was necessary, and then conditions in the cab of the *third* engine going through the single-line tunnels were not pleasant. In working westbound freight trains of around 2,000 tons up the Beaver Hill *four* 2–10–4 locomotives were needed, two at the head end, and two pushing in the rear!

Despite these very severe conditions, the articulated locomotive was not developed in Canada, while that outstanding product of the British locomotive building industry, the Beyer-Garratt, never 'caught on', as the saying goes, in North America at all. But else-where in the world many large and successful examples of this great basic design were at work. Some of the very finest exports took place after the end of the Second World War, when the fortunes of the steam locomotive were otherwise very much on the decline. The merit of the Beyer-Garratt type of locomotive is that it permits of the use of a boiler of ideal proportions for free steaming: a short barrel, and large diameter, and of a wide firebox. Mounted on the central cradle the boiler is clear of all the running gear, while the firebox is readily accessible for fire-cleaning at intermediate points on the journey, if necessary. Furthermore, the balanced symmetry of the wheel-arrangement, and equality of axle-loading gives the locomotive better tracking qualities than the Mallet type of articula-tion, as well as greater flexibility for negotiating the severe curves found in many parts of the world, in the developing countries, on sub-standard rail gauges. The evolution of the Beyer-Garratt loco-motive on the South African Railways alone is one of the epics of motive-power history.

Reference has been made earlier to the locomotive practice of the Pennsylvania Railroad and to the success of its celebrated 'K4' Pacifics. Strange though it may seem, this early development, punctuated strikingly as early as 1915, virtually ceased then so far as passenger locomotives were concerned, though some outstanding freight and mixed traffic types were introduced, of the 2–10–0 and 4–8–2 wheel arrangements, and built subsequently in large quanti-ties. When eventually this railway determined to introduce a much larger express passenger type than the 'Pacific' it took the 4–4–4–4 wheel arrangement, with four cylinders, all outside, driving two independent sets of four-coupled wheels. In effect it was comparable to the 4–8–4s of other American rail roads, but by dividing the drive it avoided the huge outside cylinders otherwise necessary. Those of the Santa Fé, for example, were 28 in. diameter by 32 in. stroke, whereas the cylinders of the Pennsylvania 4–4–4–4 were 19¾ in. diameter by 26 in. stroke. This latter railroad built a number of non-articulated 4-cylinder locomotives, including the enormous 6–4–4–6 shown at the New York World Fair in 1939, and mixed-traffic giants of the 4–6–4–4, and 4–4–6–4 type, but apart from the express passenger 4–4–4–4 of 1942, built by Baldwin, none became anything of a standard class. Even the last mentioned had a relatively short life because of the rapid advance of the diesel in North America after the end of the Second World War.

By the mid-1930s the 3 ft. 6 in. gauge Japanese National Railways were becoming completely saturated. The rapid increase in the population of the country and developing industrialism was imposing upon the railways traffic far greater than they had been built to carry. The original main lines, built on meandering alignments and at minimum cost, had been improved to a considerable extent; but speeds much in excess of 60 m.p.h. were quite exceptional. Even before the Second World War an entirely new network on the 4 ft. 8½ in. gauge was being planned. All this, however, was halted by subsequent events, and at the end of the war such was the amount of reconstruction to be carried out that recourse was made to the simplest and cheapest form of railway motive power, while plans for more ambitious developments matured. In 1948 the most powerful of all Japanese express passenger steam locomotives was introduced, the 'C 62' class 4–6–4. They were designed for heavy main-line work on the non-electrified portions of the line, and although their sphere of activity was gradually reduced, particularly after the opening of the super-speed New Tokaido Line in 1964, they had a strenuous life of around twenty-five years.

The distinction of owning the largest and heaviest steam locomotives ever to be built belongs to the Union Pacific Railroad. While the Mallet type of articulated locomotive was originally conceived as a compound and generally remained so until the end of the 1920s, the need in the U.S.A. for fast freight locomotives of exceptional capacity led to much study towards improving the riding of the large articulated types, so that speeds of 50–60 m.p.h. could be attained with safety. The majority of existing articulated locomotives often became unstable at over 25 m.p.h. It was in 1936 that the 4–6–6–4 wheel arrangement was adopted for some new locomotives for the Union Pacific. In these the weight distribution was so arranged that the front engine unit carried about 90 per cent of the weight on the back unit, and this with front boiler supports having flat surfaces, and the superior guiding influence of a leading four-wheeled bogie, made these engines the most stable-riding Mallets ever built. The compound system of working had also been

31

abandoned, and all four cylinders took live steam from the huge boiler. Even this was not enough for the Union Pacific, and in 1941 the American Locomotive Company built the colossal 4–8–8–4 'Big Boys' for this railroad. The engine alone weighed 345 Imperial tons, and the 14-wheeled tenders another 194 tons.

Sheer bigness is not necessarily a measure of effectiveness in service, and the distinction of the finest ever of British passenger locomotives will probably always be a matter of debate among enthusiasts whose personal interests favour one or another of the 'Big Four' companies of pre-nationalisation days. One had the choice between the Great Western 'Kings', the Southern air-smoothed 'Merchant Navy' 4–6–2s, several varieties of 'Pacifics' on the London and North Eastern Railway, and finally the Stanier 'Pacifics' of the LMSR. It was one of the latter, of the non-streamlined 'Duchess' series, that produced the highest recorded rate of sustained evaporation in the boiler ever registered in scientific testing in Great Britain, and in many other respects the 'Duchess' class can be considered the highest development of the British express passenger locomotive. While not wishing to accord them the premier place, they can certainly be classed among the great locomotives of all time. I have ridden many thousands of miles on their footplates and have the most vivid and pleasant memories of these journeys.

The comparison between the relative sizes of British and North American locomotives was high-lighted on two memorable occasions: first at the centenary celebrations of the Baltimore and Ohio Railroad, in 1927, at which Great Britain was represented by the GWR 4–6–0 *King George V* and in 1939 at the New York World Fair, when the LMSR streamlined Pacific *Coronation* was displayed. These expositions emphasised not only the mere size but also the additional height and width that the Americans could use, particularly as the Canadian National Railway paraded their great 'Confederation' 4–8–4 immediately behind the *King George V* in 1927. From that time eight-coupled passenger locomotives became the normal form of power on the Transcontinental expresses of the CNR. Unlike the Canadian Pacific, the former route through the Rockies involved no gradients exceptional enough to require special motive power, and the through trains were operated by a single locomotive on each stage. The 4–8–2 type was developed concurrently with the

4–8–4, and some splendid designs were produced, several examples of both having fortunately been preserved.

In many countries the latter days of the steam locomotive showed a tendency to use general-purpose rather than special types. There is the remarkable case of India, where no more than two types, 4–6–2 and 2–8–2, have been built as standard for the broad-gauge lines since the time of Independence. The Rhodesia Railways also provide a striking example in their use of the 'Beyer-Garratt' type. In 1940 delivery was taken of four locomotives of the 4–6–4 + 4–6–4 wheel arrangement, intended for working the mail trains over the 'Cape-to-Cairo' line from Bulawayo southwards into what was then the Bechuanaland Protectorate, now Botswana. But these locomotives proved so versatile, in both passenger and goods service, that in post-war years the type became a main-line standard for all classes of duty except the very heavy mineral hauls northwards over the Victoria Falls bridge into what was then Northern Rhodesia, now Zambia. These fine engines, which are described in some detail beside their picture, are among the finest-ever British locomotive exports.

The Rhodesia Railways operate on the 'Cape' gauge of 3 ft. 6 in., and on the more northerly African system in Kenya and Uganda, on the metre gauge; the development of the Beyer-Garratt type of locomotive has been little less striking. On this network, now known as the East African Railways, it was not possible to effect such a degree of standardisation as in Rhodesia. While practically the entire railway runs through wild undeveloped country, much of it thick tropical jungle, both the physical conditions and the traffic differ considerably east and west of Nairobi. Down to the east coast, at Mombasa, the line is being worked almost to maximum capacity, and it is laid with heavy rails that permit of axle loads up to 20 tons, whereas on the western stretches of the line, extending to the westernmost frontiers of Uganda, there is a strict limitation of loading. On these sections, however, traffic is not so heavy, and at the present time diesel-electric locomotives are gradually replacing the old and lighter classes of Beyer-Garratt. East of Nairobi, the enormous 59th class prevail, the largest and most powerful locomotives ever to run on metre-gauge tracks.

Out of the devastation of the Second World War the Japanese

National Railways evolved a range of new standard locomotives, of which the 'C 62' 4–6–4 mentioned earlier was the largest and most powerful. The basic features of the new range had been largely determined before the war, with the production in 1936 of the 'D 51' class of 2–8–2 freight engine, having 'Boxpok' cast-steel driving-wheel centres, and a continuous casing along the boiler top from the chimney rearwards to include the sandbox and the steam dome. These, however, were no more than externals. The design as a whole was ultra-modern, providing ready accessibility to all working parts, large bearing surfaces, and every feature conducive to high availability in traffic, and long mileages between visits to main works for overhaul. In addition to this 2–8–2 there were 2–6–0s, and a 'Pacific' in the same general series, though the latter, the 'C 55' class appearing in 1935, were not so highly developed as the other types. It was just before the war that the very fine 'C 57' class was first produced, and many additional engines of the class were built from 1946 onwards.

The metre-gauge system in India forms a large and important part of the national network, and at the same time as the new broad-gauge standard locomotive designs were produced, an equivalent, and equally attenuated, range for the metre gauge was developed – again consisting of only two types, 4–6–2 for passenger and 2–8–2 for mixed traffic and freight. Both types have been extensively built both in India and by contractors, and on the principal metre-gauge lines they are nowadays seen to the virtual exclusion of all others. This has not been to the liking of all railway enthusiasts, because the metre-gauge lines of India have in the past been worked by a great variety of interesting and picturesque older designs now rapidly disappearing. Some of these of the 4–4–0, 0–6–0, and 2–6–0 types with massive outside frames recall the time, now more than seventy years ago, when there were vaguely held ideas that some of the metre-gauge lines would be converted to broad gauge, and the locomotives also; but today, when one major conversion in the south, in the state of Kerala, is actually in process, there will be plenty of broad-gauge locomotives to take over, made redundant elsewhere by the extension of electrification and the steady replacement of steam by diesels.

It is perhaps appropriate that the last picture in this book should be of the last design of steam locomotive to be introduced in the country of its origin. Not all enthusiasts, nor yet all regular travellers by train welcomed the nationalisation of the British railways in 1948; and the range of new standard locomotives introduced from 1951 onwards had a distinctly mixed welcome from the men who had to use them. But seen in retrospect, the standard locomotives, in their various power classifications, represent a notable milestone in the history of railway motive development. It was perhaps no more than natural that the areas represented by some of the greatest and most individual of the old companies showed the strongest resentment to the products of nationalisation; but everywhere there were enginemen and running superintendents broad enough in their outlook to accept the standard types on their merits. So far as the 'Britannia' mixed-traffic 4–6–2s were concerned, perhaps their finest work was on the Great Eastern line, between London and Norwich, and on the Irish Mails, between London and Holyhead. But whatever mixed feelings there may have been about the 'Britannia' 4–6–2s and the smaller classes, the '9F' 2–10–0 seemed to have the warmest welcome everywhere, and it was certainly fitting that the very last steam locomotive to be built for service on British Railways should have been of this class – and named, significantly, *Evening Star*.

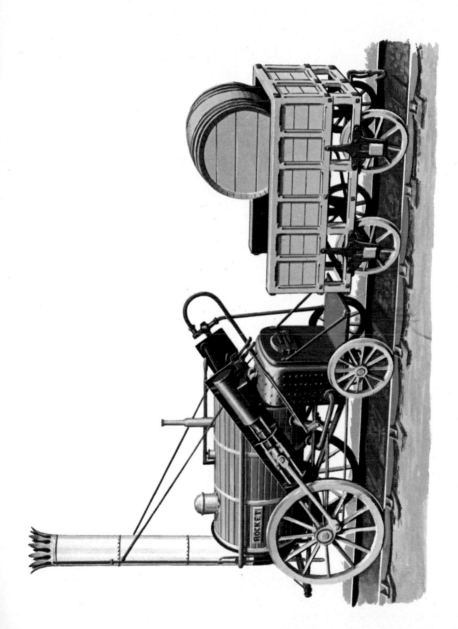

1. The *Rocket*: Liverpool and Manchester Railway, 1829.

2. The 'American' type: *Seminole* – 1867.

3. **Great Western Railway:** a Gooch 2-2-2.

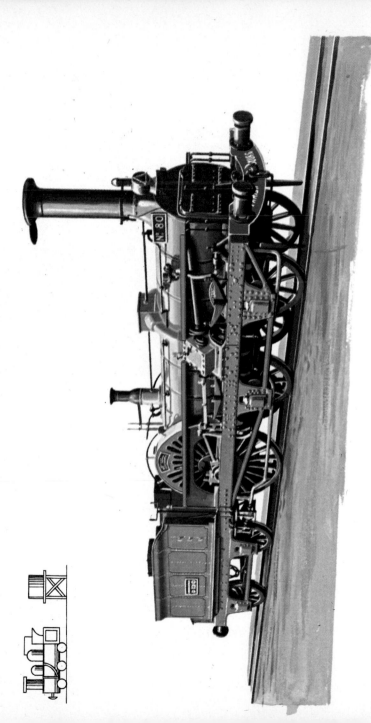

4. **Eastern Railway of France:** a 'Crampton'.

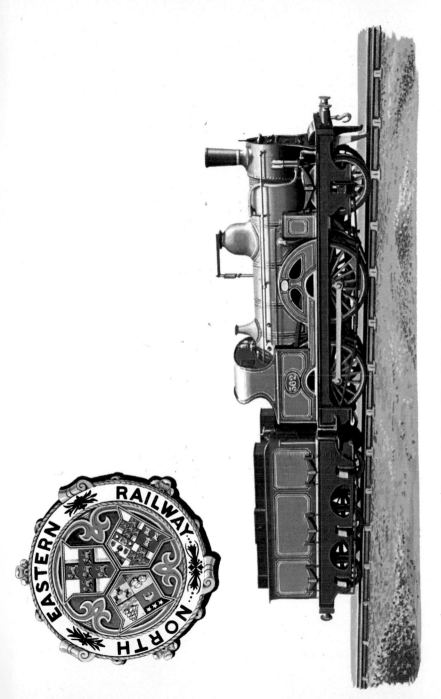

5.   North Eastern Railway: Edward Fletcher's '901', Class 2-4-0.

6. **Paris–Orleans Railway:** V. Forquenot's 2-4-2 express locomotive of 1873.

7. London, Brighton and South Coast Railway: a 'Gladstone' type 0-4-2.

8. New South Wales Government Railways: the 'P6' class 4-6-0 of 1892.

9. **Atlantic City Railroad:** A Vauclain four-cylinder compound 'Atlantic'.

10. **Dutch Rhenish Railway:** the 'Rhine Bogie' express passenger 4-4-0.

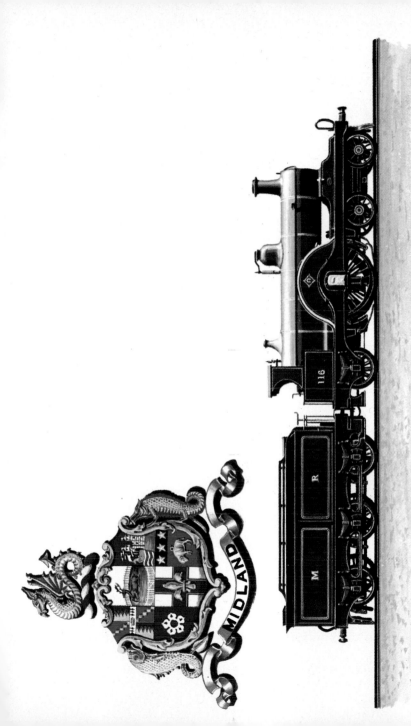

11. **Midland Railway:** Johnson's 7 ft 9 in. 4-2-2 express locomotive.

12.   **Rhodesia Railways:** the 7th class 4-8-0.

13. **Paris, Lyons and Mediterranean:** four-cylinder compound 4-4-0.

14.   **Caledonian Railway:** the 'Dunalastair' class 4-4-0 locomotive.

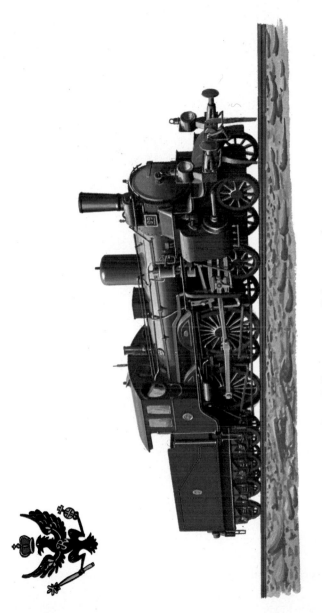

15. **Prussian State Railways:** a two-cylinder compound 4-4-0.

16.   **Canadian Pacific Railway:** the 'D 10' 4-6-0.

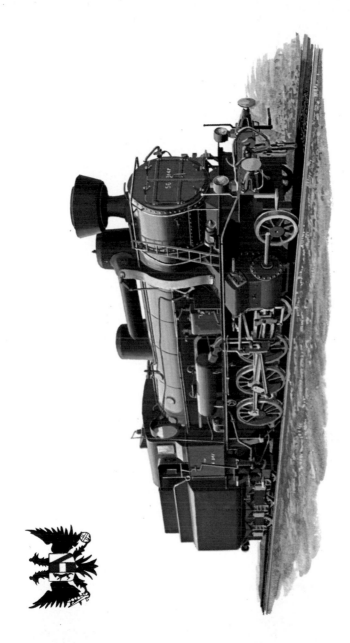

17. **Imperial Royal Austrian State Railways:** a Golsdorf compound 2-8-o.

18. **Madras and Southern Mahratta Railway:** a B.E.S.A. standard 4-4-0.

19. **Paris-Orleans Railway:** de Glehn compound 'Atlantic'.

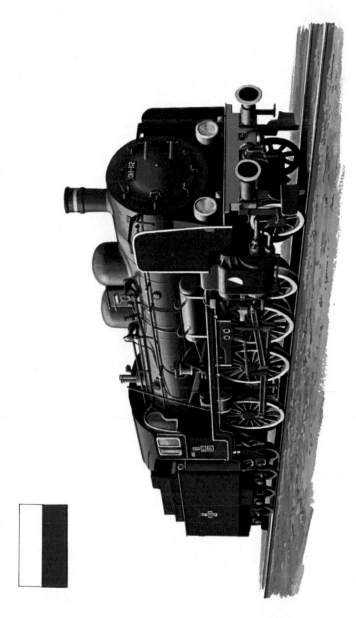

20. **Prussian State Railways:** the 'P8' 4–6–0 mixed traffic locomotive.

21. **Darjeeling Himalayan Railway:** 0-4-0 Saddle tank locomotive.

22. **Imperial Royal Austrian State Railways:** a Golsdorf four-cylinder compound 2-6-4.

23.   **Eastern Railway of France:** four-cylinder compound express 4-6-0.

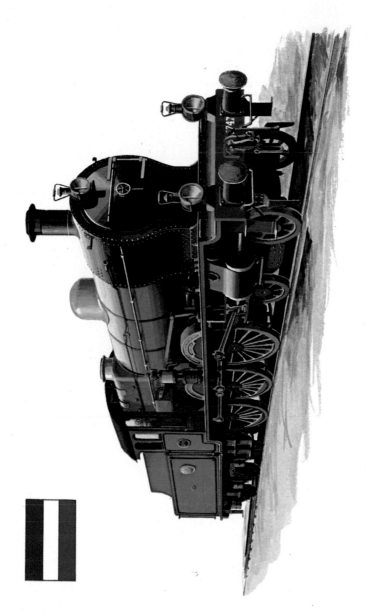

24. **Netherlands State Railways:** four-cylinder simple express 4-6-0 locomotive.

25. **London and North Western Railway:** the *Coronation* of 1911, 5,000th locomotive built at Crewe works.

26. **Brunig Railway, Switzerland:** Rack and adhesion o-6-o locomotive.

27.   **Bavarian State Railway:** the Maffei four-cylinder compound 'Pacific' class S3/6.

28. **Belgian National Railways:** the Flamme four-cylinder simple 'Pacific' of 1910.

29. **Lake Shore and Michigan Southern:** a fast express 4-6-0.

30. **New Zealand Government Railways:** the 'Ab' class 'Pacific' locomotive.

31. **Great Northern Railway (England):** the large boilered 'Atlantic'.

32. **Canadian Northern Railway:** a G-16-a class 4-6-0, in CNR livery.

33. **Southern Railway (England):** the 'King Arthur' class 4-6-0.

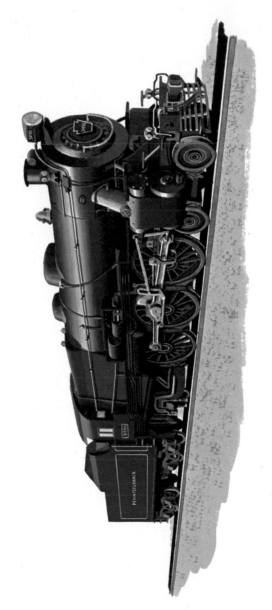

34. **Pennsylvania Railroad:** the 'K4' class Pacific.

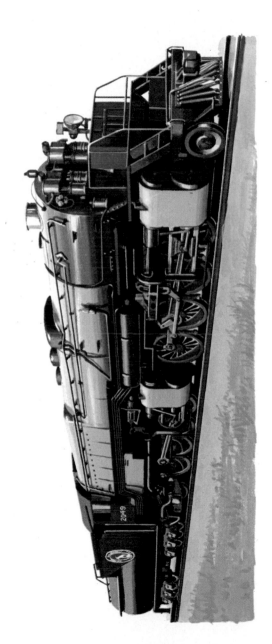

35.   **Great Northern Railway (U.S.A.):** Mallet articulated 2-8-8-2 freight locomotive.

36. **Northern Railway of France:** a Breville 'super-Pacific' of 1922.

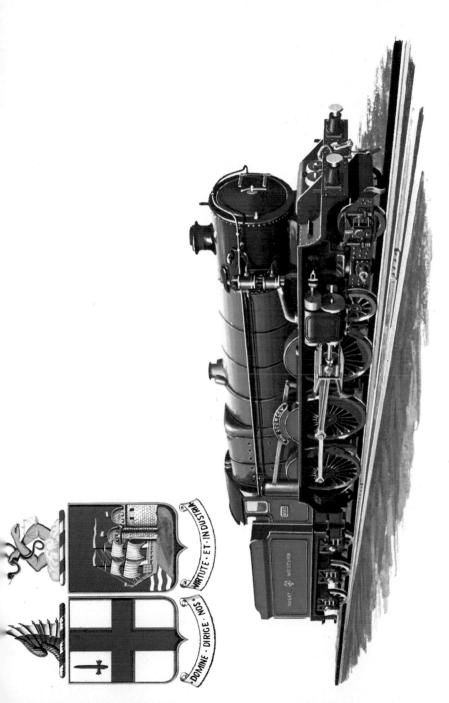

37. **Great Western Railway (England):** the 'King' class four-cylinder 4-6-0.

38.   **South African Railways:** the Class '15F' 4-8-2 express, and fast goods locomotive.

39. **Indian broad gauge standard:** 2-8-2 heavy freight locomotive, Class 'XD'.

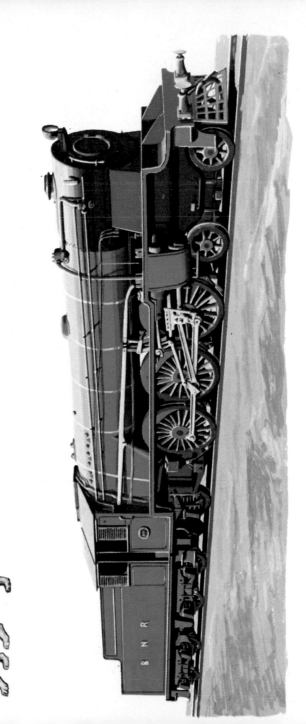

40. **Bengal Nagpur Railway:** four-cylinder de Glehn compound Pacific.

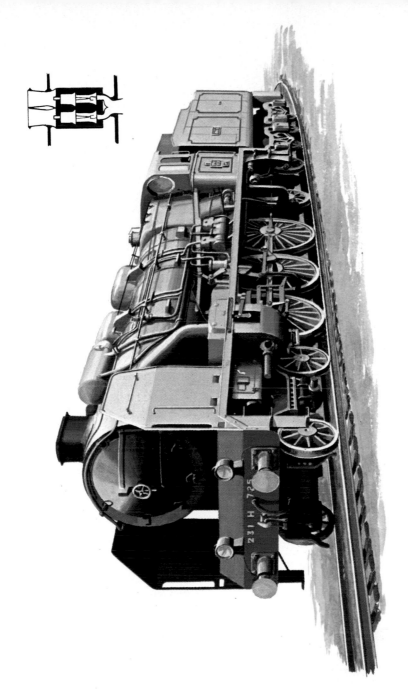

41. **Paris–Orleans Railway:** successor to the epoch-marking Pacific No. 3566.

42. **South Australian Railways:** Shea's giant 4-8-4 locomotive.

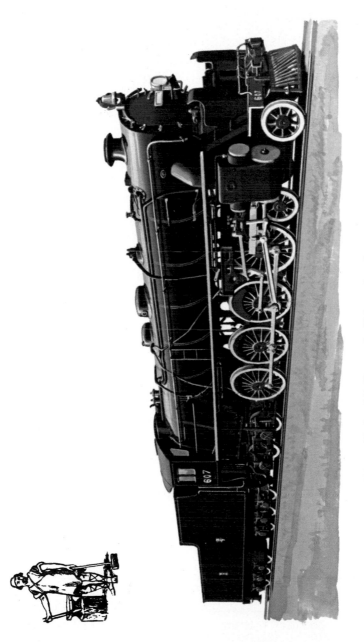

43. **Chinese National Railways:** the Vulcan 4-8-4 of 1935.

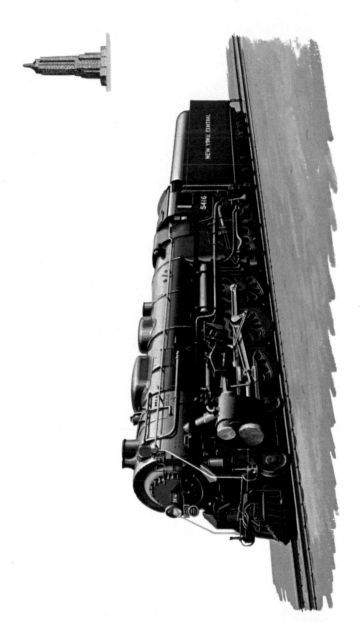

44.　New York Central: the J3a 'Hudson' 4-6-4.

45. **London and North Eastern Railway:** the record holding 'A4' class streamlined Pacific.

46. **Chicago, Milwaukee, St. Paul and Pacific Railroad:** Streamlined 4-6-4 for the 'Hiawatha' express.

47. **Canadian Pacific Railway:** the 'Royal Hudson' 4-6-4 locomotive.

48.   **Great Southern Railways (Ireland):** the three-cylinder 4-6-o express locomotive *Maeve*.

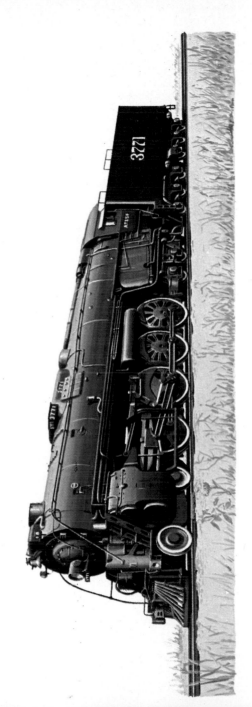

49. Atchison, Topeka and Santa Fe: a '3765' class 4-8-4.

50. **German State Railways (Reichsbahn):** the Series '52' Austerity war locomotive.

51. **French National Railways (SNCF):** the 141 R 2-8-2: L'Americaine.

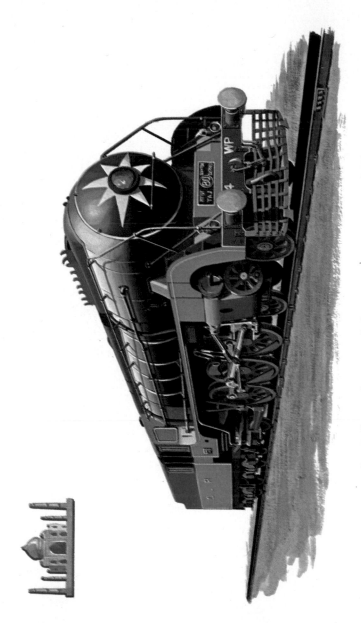

52. **Indian Railways:** the new standard express passenger 4-6-2, type 'WP'.

53. **Canadian Pacific Railway:** the 'Selkirk' 2-10-4 for Rocky Mountain service.

54. **South African Railways:** the 'GMAM' Beyer-Garratt 4-8-2 + 2-8-4 locomotive.

55.   **Pennsylvania Railroad:** the 'T1' 4-4-4-4 non-articulated high speed locomotive of 1942.

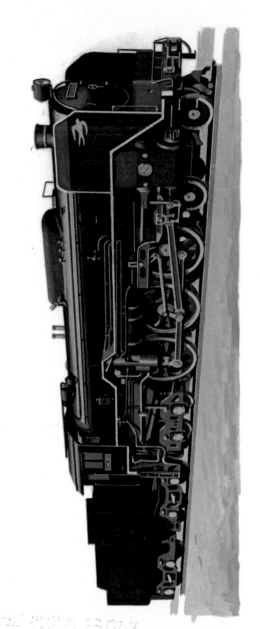

56. **Japanese National Railways:** the 'C62' class 4-6-4 express passenger locomotive.

57. **Union Pacific Railroad:** the 4-8-8-4 express freight locomotive of 1941 – 'Big Boy'.

58. **British Railways:** London Midland Region – the 'Duchess' class 4-6-2 locomotive.

59. **Canadian National Railways:** the restored 4-8-2 locomotive No. 6060.

60.   **Rhodesia Railways:** the '15A' class 4-6-4 + 4-6-4 Beyer-Garratt locomotive.

61. **East African Railways:** the '59' class 4-8-2 + 2-8-4 Beyer-Garratt locomotive.

62. **Japanese National Railways:** the 'C57' class light Pacific locomotive.

63. **Indian Railways:** the 'YG' standard metre gauge 2-8-2 freight engine.

64.   **British Railways:** the last steam locomotive built, the '9F' 2-10-0 *Evening, Star.*

THE PLATE
DESCRIPTIONS

1. The *Rocket*, Liverpool and Manchester Railway, 1829

While George Stephenson was heavily engaged in the building of the Liverpool and Manchester Railway things were not going well in his absence on the Stockton and Darlington. He had left his faithful foreman of locomotives, Timothy Hackworth, in charge of motive power, and the early steam locomotives like the pioneer *Locomotion* of 1825 did not steam freely. Hackworth did some redesigning on his own account, but in the meantime news of these troubles spread rapidly, and there was a strong body of opinion in favour of using cable traction on the Liverpool and Manchester. Fortunately more progressive ideas prevailed, and the directors offered a prize for the most suitable type of steam locomotive to work the line. George Stephenson and his son Robert did not approve of Hackworth's expedient to make locomotives steam more freely – namely the return flue, which meant that the

stoking had to be done from the chimney end of the boiler. The solution to the problem, first embodied in Robert Stephenson's entry for the Rainhill prize, was the multi-tubular boiler, and it was suggested, not by an engineer but by Henry Booth, the secretary of the railway company. It was so outstandingly successful that every steam locomotive boiler built since was like it. Another feature of the *Rocket*, which won the prize for Robert Stephenson, was the separate firebox, separate that is from the boiler barrel. This again was developed into a standard design. In the event the *Rocket* was the only entry for the Rainhill trials that fulfilled all the conditions. Its principles of design were so fundamental as to form the basis for the entire development of the steam locomotive, over more than 130 years.

2. The 'American' type: Seminole – 1867

In the early days of railways locomotive construction in the

U.S.A. was entirely by private builders, and unlike the situation that developed in Great Britain, it remained so. By the year 1845 four firms, Baldwin, Norris, Rogers, and Hinkley were supplying roughly two-thirds of the total American production of locomotives for home service and for export, and design and technical development was virtually exclusive to these manufacturers. The pioneer railways then had little choice but to take the standard products of one or other of the builders. In this situation the builders themselves developed an interesting and picturesque way of marketing their wares. These early locomotives were lavishly decorated, and beautiful coloured lithographs were produced, which the builders' representatives would take to a railway, and say, in as many words, 'How would you like a few of these?' *Seminole* is a superb example of a 4-4-0 built by the Rogers Locomotive Machine Works in 1867 for the Union Pacific Railroad. It was typical of the civil war period in the U.S.A., not only that but equally typical of 20,000 engines of the type built between 1840 and 1890. The boiler centre was low and the engine easily adapted itself to the uneven tracks of the nineteenth century. The deep firebox set down between the frames and the driving axles was ideal for wood burning, and in good firing conditions the engine would develop 350–400 horsepower. The highly decorative finish, with brass trim, scroll work, and landscape paintings on the sand box and the headlight are characteristic of the period.

3. Great Western Railway: a Gooch 2–2–2

Daniel Gooch was no more than 21 years of age when Brunel appointed him Locomotive Superintendent of the Great Western Railway in 1837, and after taking the measure of a rather freakish set of locomotives that had already been ordered, and making some important adjustments to the Stephenson-built 2–2–2 *North Star*, he designed his own express passenger 2–2–2, of which no fewer than sixty-two were ordered, from a number of contractors. These engines, known as the 'Firefly' class, could be described as enlarged and improved 'North Stars'. They were without much question the fastest and most powerful passenger engines in the world at the time of their introduction, in 1840. They had the outside 'sandwich' type of frame, oak, with a wrought-iron plate strapped on each side, and did some remarkable running at the time that the Royal Commission on Railway Gauges was in session. But perhaps the most remarkable achievement was by the engine pictured herewith, the *Actaeon*. In May 1844 when the line had been opened throughout to Exeter, Gooch himself drove this engine with a special train through from London, 193½ miles; and having joined in the great celebration lunch he drove the *Actaeon* back to London in 4 hours 40 minutes – a wonderful average for that period, of 41½ m.p.h. On favourable sections of the line the speed exceeded 60 m.p.h., and other engines of the class regularly ran at the same speed.

4. Eastern Railway of France: a 'Crampton'

The Crampton type of locomotive, invented by an Englishman, and first seen on British tracks, never attained any degree of popularity until it was introduced on to the continent of Europe. The underlying principle behind its design can be readily appreciated from the picture of *Le Continent*, the famous example that the French have most fortunately preserved, and which is now on display in the railway museum at Mulhouse, Alsace. The great 'sternwheeler' layout enables a large boiler to be mounted with its centre line relatively low, and the resulting low centre of gravity counteracted any tendency to roll, a trait that was evident in many contemporary British locomotives in which the boiler had to be mounted high enough to clear the driving-wheel axle. Crampton put the driving wheels entirely to the rear of the boiler and firebox. The type became very popular in France, at a time when train speeds were not very high, and one could jog steadily along at 40 m.p.h. or so. In England the higher speeds resulted in 'hard' riding that was kind neither to the track nor to the men on the engine. A feature of *Le Continent* that will be noted is that not only were the cylinders beside the boiler, partly concealed by the outside framing, but the valve gear was also outside. The eccentrics of the Stephenson's link motion can be seen beside the driving-wheel boss.

5. North Eastern Railway: Edward Fletcher's '901', Class 2–4–0

Among nineteenth-century engineers who had literally grown up with the steam locomotive there was no more remarkable nor endearing personality than Edward Fletcher, for twenty-nine years Locomotive Superintendent of the North Eastern Railway. He was an apprentice at Stephenson's works when the *Rocket* was built; he drove the *Invicta* at the opening of the Canterbury and Whitstable Railway in 1830, and by the time he took charge of the N.E.R. at the age of 47 he had amassed a wealth of practical experience in the building and running of locomotives that was worth a lifetime of book-learning. Furthermore, he had a way of handling men that inspired an almost fanatic loyalty from one of the toughest groups of railwaymen that could then be imagined. With them what 'Th' 'auld mon' did was right: there was no argument about it! They had good reason for their confidence in him. His locomotives were not only positive works of art, to behold, as can be appreciated from the Meadway painting; they were free running, light on coal, and were so soundly constructed they they gave no trouble in service. The '901' class, the first of which was built at Gateshead Works in 1872, was his masterpiece, and it is indeed fortunate that one of them has been preserved, and is on display at the Railway Museum at York. She represents perhaps the very height of elegance reached by British locomotives in the nineteenth century.

6. Paris–Orleans Railway: V. Forquenot's 2–4–2 express locomotive of 1873

Until the end of the nineteenth century the French railways, taken collectively, were not renowned for speed. The parcelling out of definite territorial limits for each of the companies virtually eliminated competition, and with guaranteed dividends there was little incentive to improve train services. The Orleans company, however, was an exception. In the south the Midi railway controlled all the routes into Spain, but there were two competitive routes from Paris, the Orleans, and the Paris, Lyons and Mediterranean. The Midi encouraged the former, because interchange with the Orleans at Bordeaux gave them a longer mileage of the international traffic than that from the PLM, at Cette. In consequence, the Orleans ran some splendid trains from Paris to Bordeaux, and between 1873 and 1894 the engines hauling them were Forquenot's 2–4–2s – about the best passenger locomotives in France in the pre-compound era. They were as striking in appearance, with their brass-jacketed boilers, as they were good at their job; and no fewer than 397 of them were built. Even with the introduction of progressively larger engines in the twentieth century, culminating in Chapelon's work in the 1930s, duties were still found for these great little 2–4–2s, and some of them, of the smaller-wheeled variety, remained in service until 1949. One of them restored to all its original gleaming glory is preserved in the Railway Museum at Mulhouse.

7. London, Brighton and South Coast Railway: a 'Gladstone' type 0–4–2

Studying the painting of *Fratton* it is not difficult to understand why railway enthusiasts of the nineteenth century verily worshipped at the feet of William Stroudley. The colour of his engines was enough attraction in itself, yet curiously enough its official description was 'improved engine green'. It was not reserved exclusively for express passenger locomotives; it was only the slow goods engines that were not so favoured. One with an eye on maintenance might have thought it a rather unpractical livery for suburban tank engines working in the smoky atmosphere of south-east London and the line through the Thames Tunnel. But that was partly Stroudley's idea: it *would* show the dirt – and in those days on the Brighton woe betide the driver whose engine was not spotless! The naming was not very imaginative. Every town, village, and hamlet on the line had some kind of engine named after it, and while some of the 'Gladstones' were named after directors, statesmen, and other dignitaries, recourse had to be made to stations to fill in the gaps, and of these *Fratton* was one, a suburb of Portsmouth, where there was a large Brighton engine shed. The engines all had their own drivers, and no other, and the driver's name was painted on the inside of the cab. Presumably care would have to be taken to allocate *Gladstone* to a gentleman whose political sympathies were Liberal, and that *Beaconsfield* was driven by a staunch Conservative!

8. New South Wales Government Railways: the 'P6' class 4-6-0 of 1892

It was not surprising that Beyer, Peacock & Co. had grave doubts about the 'P6' engines. They were by far the largest and heaviest that had yet been built in Great Britain, and in New South Wales where they were some 20 tons heavier than the previous standard 4-4-0s, and 13 tons more than the generally unpopular '373' class of 4-4-0, they created something of a sensation. But their free steaming and easy riding soon endeared them to the enginemen, and their great power made them invaluable on the heavily graded routes. From the first order for fifty, their numbers were increased until, by 1911, no fewer than 191 were in service. The wheel spacing was unusual, and the long distance between the second and third pairs of coupled wheels was in order to accommodate a deep firebox, largely at Dugald Drummond's recommendation. New South Wales coal was very like Scottish in its

burning characteristics, and despite its indifferent quality, by the best English and Welsh standards, Drummond's engines on the Caledonian were notably free steamers. Another Scottish feature, though not one used by Drummond, was the Allan straight-link valve gear – considered by some to be the best of all gears of the link-motion type. In later years the 'P6' engines were rebuilt with superheaters, still further increasing their efficiency. But perhaps the greatest tribute to the design came in 1917, when it was adopted without alteration for the Commonwealth Railways Trans-Australian line from Port Augusta to Kalgoorlie, including the famous 297-mile 'straight' across the Nullarbor Plain.

9. Atlantic City Railroad: a Vauclain 4-cylinder compound 'Atlantic'

In the U.S.A. the need for larger fireboxes led to the development of the very popular 'American' type, or 4-4-0 with outside cylinders, into the 4-4-2 to enable larger fireboxes to be mounted clear of the driving wheels. It was in 1894 that the first locomotive of this type was built, for the Atlantic Coast

Line, and the type thereafter became known as the 'Atlantic'. It was subsequently adopted by the Atlantic City Railroad for running what was sometimes claimed to be the fastest train in the world in regular service. In 1897 it was booked to cover the 55½ miles from Camden station, Philadelphia, to Atlantic City in 52 minutes, and there are many stories of the run being made in considerably shorter time. The locomotives that ran the Atlantic City flyers were not only very speedy in themselves; they typified two phases of American locomotive development that persisted for a long time. The first of these was the strange addiction to the 'Mother Hubbard' type of cab, half-way along the boiler. There can have been little opportunity for close collaboration between driver and fireman, but none of the railway *littérateurs* of the day seem to have ridden in the cabs on these locomotives, and first-hand accounts of what the experience was like are lacking. The other feature was the use of the Vauclain system of compounding with the high- and low-pressure cylinders mounted one above the other, and their pistons connected to a common cross-head.

10. Dutch Rhenish Railway: the 'Rhine Bogie' express passenger 4-4-0

It might seem strange that to represent so very British a locomotive type as the inside-cylinder inside-framed, bogie, four-coupled express, that a foreign example should be chosen; but the 'Rhine Bogie', of which a beautifully restored example is preserved in the Dutch Railway Museum at Utrecht, was not only British built but would have looked completely at home on the British railways of the nineteenth century – apart from its colour scheme. The first engines of this class were built in 1889 by Sharp, Stewart & Co. in their Atlas Works, Glasgow, and they were as simple and straightforward a design as one could imagine. As it turned out, they had a very short existence in the service of the company that ordered them, because in 1890 the major part of the Dutch Rhenish Railway was absorbed into the State Railway. The rest went to the Holland Railway, and it was this latter company that took over the original nine 'Rhine Bogies'. That company had previously used rather ugly outside-cylindered 2-4-0s, mostly German built; but they were so impressed with the 'Rhine Bogies' that the design was adopted as a standard, and a further thirty-eight were added to the stock between 1891 and 1903. Some of them were still in service on light passenger trains until the Second World War, by which time the oldest of them were around fifty years old.

11. Midland Railway: Johnson's 7 ft. 9 in. 4–2–2 express locomotive

In Matthew Kirtley's time as locomotive superintendent the Midland Railway ceased building single-driver express locomotives after 1866, having regard to the constantly undulating character of most of its main lines, and all the important express work was thenceforth, for more than twenty years, entrusted to 2–4–0s, and later to 4–4–0s. Then came the invention of the steam sanding gear, and in 1887 the first of a lengthy series of 4–2–2 express engines was built at Derby. Opinions may differ, but I think this class, collectively, were among the most beautifully proportioned passenger locomotives ever built. Be-

tween 1887 and 1893 the details of design were developed, and the driving wheel diameter increased from 7 ft. 4 in. to 7 ft. 6 in., by which time there were sixty of them in service. But the climax came in 1896–97 with the production of the '115' class, with driving wheels still larger, at 7 ft. 9 in., larger boilers and cylinders. They were stationed at Nottingham, Bristol, and Kentish Town, while Derby and Birmingham had one each. They were brilliant performers, on a very low rate of coal consumption, while No. 117 was one of the only two British locomotives authentically recorded at 90 m.p.h. before the end of the nineteenth century.

12. Rhodesia Railways: the 7th class 4–8–0

To meet the conditions existing on so many of the colonising railways built in Southern Africa the 4–8–0 type was ideal. It permitted a distribution of the weight of a good-sized boiler over many axles, and as speed was of no consequence in the early days, small-diameter coupled wheels could be used, and the boiler set low, giving extra stability in running. The first examples of this type were built in 1892 for the Cape Government Railway, by Dübs & Co. of Glasgow. They were known as the 7th class, and this first delivery of six engines was followed in 1896 by thirty-two more from Neilson & Co., also of Glasgow. They were so successful that they became virtually a standard type for many railways in Africa. When the 'Cape-to-Cairo' line had advanced as far north as Bulawayo some engines of this class were hired by the Bechuanaland Railway, and others went to Rhodesia. Later, further engines were purchased new for Rhodesia, and it is one of these that has been preserved and is on display in the Railway Museum at Bulawayo. From this design was developed an extensive series of 4–8–0s, used in many Southern African countries, including the Benguela Railway, some for the Belgian Congo, built to the same design by the Société St. Leonard, of Liège, and some also for Nyasaland. Although originating as the Cape 7th class, it virtually became a Southern African standard. The device in the corner of the picture, three rails interlaced, is the present insignia of the Rhodesia Railways.

13. Paris, Lyons and Mediterranean: 4-cylinder compound 4–4–0

One of the most interesting developments of the 4-cylinder compound type of locomotive in France was on the Paris, Lyons and Mediterranean Railway. That company had some unusual problems in operation. Except for a length of roughly 100 miles between Laroche and Dijon, where the line passed through the elevated region of the Côte d'Or mountains, the gradients were easy over the rest of the 536 miles between Paris and Marseilles. Again while no very severe demands were made upon locomotive power in working the ordinary passenger service, the high-class tourist traffic, winter and summer alike, to the coastal resorts on the Côte d'Azur demanded fast and heavy trains, with every luxury that such traffic demanded. The 4-cylinder compound 4–4–0 developed on the PLM was a very successful development of the de Glehn principle, very fast because the science of steam flow had been carefully studied, and exceptionally large passages had been provided for the low-pressure cylinders. When French locomotives were not supposed to exceed 120 km/hr (74·5 m.p.h.) these PLM 4-4-0s used to attain 80 m.p.h. But while they were internally 'streamlined' their exterior was no less striking. In the south of France, in the Rhône delta, they had to combat the effects of the oft-times furious Mistral wind, and the external streamlining applied to them was described as a 'wind-cutter'. The class as a whole acquired the nickname of the 'coupe-vent' locomotives.

14. Caledonian Railway: the 'Dunalastair' class 4-4-0 locomotive

The intense rivalry between the East and West Coast routes from London to Scotland that reached a climax in the race to Aberdeen in August 1895 did not reach any clear-cut conclusion. Having attained an advantage in time roughly proportionate to their shorter mileage on the night of August 21/22, 1895, the East Coast companies gave up racing and made no further reply to the sensationally fast West Coast run on the following night. But during the winter of 1895–96, both sides seemed covertly to be preparing for a resumption of racing in the summer of 1896. It was in this uneasy period that

the epoch-making Caledonian locomotive development took place, with the production of the famous 'Dunalastairs'. The engine shown in our picture was one of the first batch, which almost 'trailed their coat-tails' to their East Coast rivals by some very fast running with the Tourist train in 1896; but the development went otherwise. Instead of needing higher speed the demand came for heavier loads, and McIntosh built more 'Dunalastairs' with still larger boilers, setting a new fashion that spread over much of Great Britain. The illustrated locomotive was named in 1897 in honour of the Diamond Jubilee of Queen Victoria, and was one of the very few Caledonian engines that ever bore names.

15. Prussian State Railways: a 2-cylinder compound 4-4-0

This type of locomotive, compounded on the von Borries system, was running the fastest trains in Germany at the turn of the century. These were allowed 113 minutes to cover the 99 miles from Hamburg to Wittenberge, where engines were changed. From there the remaining 78¾ miles to Berlin were run in 91 minutes – in both cases average speeds of around 52 m.p.h. over an easy road. This was the route over which the spectacular 'Flying Hamburger' diesel train was put on in the 1930s. On the Prussian 4-4-0s the cylinders were outside, and had the slide valves mounted above them, actuated by Walchaerts gear. At that time the track was of fairly light formation, and these locomotives were built with the style of suspension that was universal in America at one time, with compensating beams between the coupled axles to provide a three-point suspension. At that time also speed was officially limited to 90 km (56 m.p.h.) and had this been strictly kept it would not have been possible to maintain booked time, and speed usually had to be 61 or 62 m.p.h. over much of the route. Because of the three-point suspension, the engines rode reasonably well on the very light track.

16. Canadian Pacific Railway: the 'D 10' 4-6-0

In view of its almost universal application in the U.S.A., it was not surprising that the Canadian Pacific Railway began operations with the popular American type 4-4-0; but the exceptional gradients in British Columbia required something more powerful, and early in the present century the 4-6-0 type was adopted for general passenger and fast freight work. The 'D 10' class was introduced in 1905, and quickly attained great popularity by its simple, robust design, and the reliability it had in heavy service. Their technical characteristics were a large, free-steaming boiler, large cylinders, and coupled wheels of 5 ft. 3 in. diameter. Looking at the picture it might be a little difficult to realise this latter dimension; but the great height to which Canadian locomotives can be built – taken full advantage of in the 'D 10' – can give a false impression of the driving-wheel size. The earlier engines of the class had their valves actuated by inside Stephenson link motion; but in No. 1057, illustrated, the gear is Walschaerts, with piston valves. In all 502 engines of the 'D 10' class were built between 1905 and 1913. The shield in the top left-hand corner of the picture is that of Saskatchewan, one of the great prairie provinces of Canada, from which the CPR has always derived much traffic.

17. Imperial Royal Austrian State Railways: a Gölsdorf compound 2-8-0

There are certain routes among the railways of the world that have verily dictated locomotive policy, and the way eastward from Switzerland into Austria via the Arlberg Tunnel is one of these. When confronted with long gradients of 1 in 32 and 1 in 38 it is a case of 'all or nothing' so far as locomotives are concerned; and it was in designing for the haulage of passenger trains over this route that Karl Gölsdorf introduced his famous system of compounding in 1897 on the 2-8-0 type '170' class. These were a development of his first essay in two-stage expansion, which had been made on some 4-4-0s in 1894; but the '170' class was to be a mighty weight hauler. Part of their outstanding success came from the simplicity in handling. Gölsdorf used no special starting valve. Providing the slide valves were set in full gear, steam from the boiler could enter the low-pressure cylinder direct through two small ports, formed through 'bridges' placed across the normal admission ports of the low-pressure cylinder. It was only when the valves were in full gear that these small ports were uncovered. Directly linking up began, the low-pressure cylinder received steam only from the exhaust of the high-pressure, in normal compound working. The '170' class, originally designed as a passenger type for the Arlberg route, was later built extensively as a freight-type for general service in Austria.

18. Madras and Southern Mahratta Railway: a B.E.S.A. standard 4-4-0

The M. & S.M. was one of the many dual-gauge railways in India, though in this particular case the situation arose out of an amalgamation, rather than of the policy of building metre-gauge feeder lines to the main broad-gauge network, as in the case, for example, of the Bombay Baroda and Central India. On the railway now under review the Madras Railway – one of the first authorised in India – was a broad-gauge line, whereas the Southern Mahratta was metre gauge. In its amalgamated form the M. & S.M. was a partner with the Great Indian Peninsula in running the important Inter-City mail service between Bombay and Madras. The locomotive shown in our picture is typical of the B.E.S.A. design, in which the traditional British 4–4–0 of sixty to seventy years ago was adapted to Indian needs. Apart from such details as the cowcatcher and cab-protection against the heat of the sun, the design was quite typical of British practice of the period, with inside cylinders, inside Stephenson's link motion, and a general neatness of outline that a connoisseur of British locomotives travelling in India would find very familiar.

19. Paris–Orleans Railway: de Glehn compound 'Atlantic'

Partly because of the very successful results from its application on 4–4–0 and 'Atlantic' locomotives of the Northern Railway of France, and no less from its great intrinsic merit, the de Glehn system of compounding had, by the early 1900s, become one of the best known of all. Earlier in this book reference has been made to the influence exerted, far beyond the frontiers of France, by the Nord 'Atlantics', but the slightly larger variety on the Paris–Orleans Railway were perhaps even more remarkable engines, and were capable of

sustained 1,800 indicated horsepower continuously, because of a superlatively good design of valves and steam passages. How good these Orleans 'Atlantics' were was emphasised in a rather unfortunate manner after the introduction of the 4-cylinder compound 'Pacifics' from 1907 onwards. These latter engines had a steaming capacity 38 per cent greater than that of the 'Atlantics', yet they could barely attain 2,000 indicated horsepower, only a 10 per cent increase. Yet it was this very disappointment with the 'Pacifics' that led to the everfamous Chapelon studies in the late 1920s. The Orleans 'Atlantics' were not only great in their own right but their very greatness sparked off a research leading to one of the greatest epochs in the history of the steam locomotive, as told in connection with our picture No. 41.

20. Prussian State Railways: the 'P8' 4–6–0 mixed traffic locomotive

This very numerous generalservice type of locomotive dates from 1906, and in its bare essentials is nothing more than a simple, straightforward 2-

cylinder 4–6–0, with outside Walschaerts, valve-gear actuating piston valves. But like many locomotive designs in that category, it was one that by its mechanical excellence and reliability became extremely popular, and during the remaining years of the Prussian State Railways, between 1906 and 1921, no fewer than 3,370 were built. As part of the Armistice terms of 1918, a total of 168 'P8' 4–6–0s were among the 2,000 locomotives handed over to Belgium as war reparations, while subsequently another 101 were built for the newly constituted German State Railways. German states other than Prussia had also adopted the design, while Rumania, Latvia, and Lithuania ordered more of them. Our picture, based on a photograph taken quite recently, shows one of the 100 purchased by the Polish State Railways. As far as can be ascertained, the total built for all European countries was 3,950 – a fine tribute to a great design.

21. Darjeeling Himalayan Railway: 0–4–0 saddle tank locomotive

The problem of designing locomotives to haul a good paying load on a railway of such exceptional physical character was no light one. The principal ascent includes a length of $16\frac{1}{2}$ miles at an average gradient of 1 in 29, with a maximum of 1 in 20. Curves are as sharp as 70 ft. radius, involving several spiral loops, and the rail gauge is no more than 2 ft. 0 in. The design of the locomotives dates back to 1889, and it is remarkable that no changes have since been made, and the line is still entirely operated by steam. From the introduction of the first two of these quaint little 0–4–0 saddle tanks in 1889 additions have been made until the last one was built, by the North British Locomotive Company, in 1927 – thirty-two in all. Of this total twenty-seven are still in service. They are tiny little things weighing no more than $15\frac{1}{2}$ tons; but they have been well maintained and continue to pound their ways up the mountain slopes. It remains one of the greatest sights for the railway enthusiast anywhere in the world, because of the spectacular engineering and magnificent scenery. Unfortunately it was not one of the easiest of railways to reach.

22. Imperial Royal Austrian State Railways: a Gölsdorf 4-cylinder compound 2-6-4

In developing his compound system from 2 to 4 cylinders Gölsdorf at once obtained a better-balanced engine, and one more suited to fast express work. While much of the State railway system included heavy gradients and severe curvature that naturally restricted maximum speeds, the main line between Salzburg and Vienna is suitable for fast running, while the line between Vienna and Prague, then entirely within the Austro-Hungarian Empire, was very much a prestige route. From the viewpoint of carrying a large firebox clear of the coupled wheels, the 2-6-4 wheel arrangement was ideal; but the idea of having greater guidance than a two-wheeled pony truck at the leading end, on a fast express engine, could not be accepted without some qualification. To provide adequate guidance at the front end Gölsdorf adopted the 'Helmholz' truck. The two leading wheels, and the first pair of driving wheels were carried on a 'bogie' of their own, capable of swivelling to suit the curves in the line, and to accom-modate this lateral movement of the leading coupled wheels in relation to the after ones, which were carried on the main frame, the coupling rods had a vertical pin joint. In all there were fifty of these splendid engines, built between 1908 and 1916.

23. Eastern Railway of France: 4-cylinder compound express 4-6-0

The Est Railway was alone among the great railways of France in using, and continuously developing, 4-6-0 types for the heaviest and fastest express work. The '3103' class had certain notable features in their basic design. They were 4-cylinder de Glehn compounds in the strictest sense. That they had the largest coupled wheels ever put on to a French six-coupled engine, 6 ft. $10\frac{1}{4}$ in., was perhaps no more than incidental; but they were not only superheated, but had a higher degree of superheating than at first became usual in France. When the earliest results of Dr. Schmidt's work on superheating became known it was in certain quarters hailed as an alternative to compounding to secure higher thermal efficiency; but on the Est the two were allied, and resulted in one of the finest locomotives of the day. There was a good deal of inter-railway testing of locomotives in the years before 1914, and Est superheated compound 4–6–os made some remarkable running on both the Nord and the Orleans main lines. But the outbreak of war put an end to these interesting exchanges. It was evident, however, that the Est 4–6–0 was practically equal in tractive ability to the much larger Orleans 'Pacifics'. A total of 138 had been built up to that time, and in 1925, when new locomotives were needed, the Est ordered another fifty, rather than design a class of 'Pacifics'.

24. Netherlands State Railways: 4-cylinder simple express 4–6–0 locomotive

The outcome of the fruitful co-operation between the civil and mechanical engineers of the Netherlands State Railways over the question of axle-loading and dynamic balancing was the production in 1910 of the splendid 4-cylinder 4–6–0 design, of which the first examples were built in England in 1910. As with so many earlier Dutch locomotives, the detail designing was done by Beyer, Peacock & Co. in Manchester, but even before the first English-built batches were completed, the Dutch firm of Werkspoor were building more of them, to the same drawings. After the First World War another thirty were built by German firms, which added to the thirty-six originals by Beyer, Peacock and the fifty-four by Werkspoor made a total of 120. As originally turned out, with polished brass dome and safety valve covers, they were delightful to look upon, but to an engineer the most appealing feature was the quiet effortless way in which they went about their work. Engine No. 3737, one of those built by Werkspoor in 1911, was restored to its original style of painting and preserved in the Railway Museum at Utrecht; but such is the present-day interest in historical steam locomotives that the engine has since been restored to full working order, and is used on occasions for enthusiasts' special trains. Engine No. 3747, the subject of our picture, is also one of the Werkspoor-built series.

25. London and North Western Railway: the *Coronation* of 1911, 5,000th locomotive built at Crewe works

When C. J. Bowen Cooke took office as Chief Mechanical Engineer, in 1909, the locomotive department was in a generally healthy state. The principal express trains had good paying loads and kept excellent time, the total revenue was considerably the highest of any British company, and the working expenses low enough for gratifying dividends to be paid. So why was there any need for larger and more powerful locomotives? But the locomotives were undoubtedly small for the work they did, and had to be driven proportionately hard, and Bowen Cooke was seeking greater efficiency. He saw the answer in high-degree superheating, but had some difficulty in obtaining authority to build locomotives that would cost more than the existing ones. In 1910 two new 4–4–0 engines were built for direct comparison, one superheated, the other not: the *George the Fifth* and the *Queen Mary*. The chassis design was the same as the non-superheated 'Precursor' class of 1904, and the *George the Fifth* not only showed a saving in fuel of 27 per cent over the rival but also displayed an astonishing enhancement in power output. Bowen Cooke thenceforth had no difficulty in obtaining authority to build many more, one of which was the famous *Coronation* of 1911, used for many special trains in that year of national celebration. In normal service the performances of these engines were the phenomena of the day, but having regard to that chassis design they were inclined to overtax their strength, a weakness that showed in rough riding when they had covered a substantial mileage since general overhaul.

26. Brünig Railway, Switzerland: Rack and adhesion 0–6–0 locomotive

Railway Museums are fascinating places on any account, and enthusiasts from far and wide travel to them to study locomotives, rolling stock, signalling of a long past era, and sometimes wish they had been born earlier so that they could have seen some of these priceless relics in revenue-earning service. But when the delights of a museum are combined with such an incomparable setting as that by the lake-side at Lucerne one's cup of happiness is indeed full. The 'Rack and Adhesion' type of locomotive, formerly the standard motive power on the Brünig Railway, is one of the most notable exhibits. It has been carefully sectioned, so that one can follow the steam circuit and see how, when on the rack sections, the exhaust steam from the cylinders driving the road wheels was diverted from the normal exhaust to drive the low-pressure cylinders providing power for the 'rack' engine. It is a superb museum piece. If one wishes to see a complete locomotive of this type in full working guise a second engine of the class has been preserved and is on display at Meiringen, on the main line over which the eighteen engines of this class formerly worked. Engines of this same basic design also worked on the Furka–Oberalp Railway, in Switzerland, and on the Ooty railway, in South India.

27. Bavarian State Railway: the Maffei 4-cylinder compound 'Pacific', class S3/6

The collaboration in engine designing between the Bavarian State Railways and the firm of Maffei of Münich was as close and fruitful as that of Alfred de Glehn and the Société Alsacienne with the French railways, and of Beyer, Peacock with the Netherlands State; and in 1908 Anton Hammel of Maffei designed the 'Pacific' that all locomotive enthusiasts would agree is both 'famous' and 'great'. Most travellers in the south of Germany will have seen these engines in the livery of the *Bundesbahn*, and one of them beautifully restored and maintained, in gleaming black with red wheels, is on display outside the present Kraus-Maffei headquarters offices outside Münich. But the *Bundesbahn*, proud of one of the finest designs inherited from the old State railway systems, restored another of them to the original all-green Bavarian livery of 1908, and presented it to the Deutsches Museum in Münich. It is this engine that is the subject of our picture, but the varied history of the whole class must be added. There were originally ninety-seven on the Bavarian State Railways; then after nationalisation of the German railways an order for a further thirty was placed with Maffei in 1923–24, and another forty were built in 1927–31. Out of this total nineteen of the original Bavarian stud were handed over as war reparations in 1919.

28. Belgian National Railways: the Flamme 4-cylinder simple 'Pacific' of 1910

Steam locomotive design is one of those arts that admits of no clear-cut and single solution to any particular problem, as one can appreciate vividly by comparison of the Gölsdorf 2–6–4 (plate 22) with the Flamme 'Pacific'. Both were designed to do much the same kind of work, and both had the problem of accommodating a very large firebox clear of the coupled wheels. French engineers, like those of the Paris–Orleans, adopted different techniques. Flamme retained the 'Pacific' wheel arrangement, putting only a single pair of wheels under his large firebox, with the result that the leading bogie went far in front of the smokebox. These Belgian 'Pacifics' were certainly not born great; neither very early in their careers had greatness thrust upon them! In fact, they were very troublesome. But with the most assiduous attention to all the points of difficulty these were gradually overcome, and as finally modified by Monsieur Legein after the First World War they became fine and reliable engines. All the same, their extraordinary shape remained, accentuated by such additions as the A.C.F.I. feed-water heater, smoke-deflecting plates and double chimneys. They had achieved greatness – but never beauty.

29. Lake Shore and Michigan Southern: a fast express 4–6–0

The 4–6–0 was a very popular type in the U.S.A., and most of the large total of 17,000 built were for intermediate and mixed-traffic duty. It was the natural development of the 'American', or 4–4–0 type, and was readily adapted to have the same good riding quality. By means of compensating suspension of the driving axles, the engine could be built with the same three-point principle of suspension. There were, however, a few exceptions to the general employment of the type, and our picture shows a particularly fine example, built by Brooks in 1900 for fast express passenger service on the Lake Shore and Michigan Southern. The basic proportions are very similar to those of the contemporary

British 4–6–0s on railways like the North Eastern and Caledonian, with 6 ft. 8 in. coupled wheels, cylinders 20 in. diameter by 28 in. stroke, and a tractive effort of 23,800 lb. At that period in the U.S.A. the Stephenson link motion was the almost universal valve gear, mounted between the frames. This engine has piston valves, and the high raised running plate and huge cab are typical of American practice; equally, of course, was the placing of the sand box on the top of the boiler barrel. All in all, the engine has a high-stepping elegant appearance.

30. New Zealand Government Railways: the 'Ab' class 'Pacific' locomotive

The 'Pacific' type of locomotive was introduced into New Zealand as early as 1901, in rather strange circumstances. A new and larger design of passenger engine was needed capable of burning the soft lignite coal of Otago, and the Baldwin Locomotive Works of Philadelphia proposed a 'Mother Hubbard' 4–6–0, with a great wide firebox overhanging the rear pair of coupled wheels. But Mr. Beattie, the locomotive superintendent, would have none of it, and specified instead a boiler with a

wide firebox entirely behind the coupled wheels, with a two-wheeled truck to support its weight. Thus was born the New Zealand 'Q' class. From this experience Beattie designed his own 'Pacifics', the 'A' class, which, believe it or not, were 4-cylinder de Glehn compounds. They did so well that a total of fifty-seven were built, between 1906 and 1914. They were essentially passenger engines, but when H. H. Jackson succeeded Beattie in 1913 he determined to produce a general-service engine that would work passenger and freight alike, and the result was the ever-memorable 'Ab' class – 2-cylinder simple, robust, utterly reliable, and a 'great' locomotive from the moment the first of the eventually numerous class took the rails in 1915. Of the 141 engines of this class two are still in working order, in superb condition for running the 'Kingston Flyer'; but one has to travel almost to the very southernmost tip of New Zealand to see them.

31. Great Northern Railway (England): the large-boilered 'Atlantic'

In the winter of 1895 Patrick Stirling died. For nearly thirty years, as Locomotive Superintendent of the G.N.R., he had been a positively legendary figure, and the appointment of any successor would be regarded with some apprehension. H. A. Ivatt, coming from Ireland to take up the post, was conscious enough of the situation, and made a statement to the men saying how he realised he was following a very great engineer, and he added: 'There will be changes, but I will see to it that you have plenty of steam.' Within a very short time his seemingly monstrous 'Atlantics' were at work, though the demands of traffic were not excessive. For once locomotive capacity had stepped well ahead of the needs of the times. But it was not for long, and although the design was introduced by Ivatt, a great deal more than mere finishing touches were added by his successor, H. N. Gresley. To a fundamentally good design was added superheating – really *high* degree superheating – which together with well-designed piston valves produced astonishing performances. In the 1930s engines intended for running 300-ton trains at 50–52 m.p.h. were occasionally taking 550-ton trains at 55 m.p.h.; and as for the Leeds Pullman trains, one of them made a net average speed over the 186 miles of 63½ m.p.h., attaining 93 m.p.h. in the process: great locomotives indeed.

32. Canadian Northern Railway: a G-16-a class 4–6–0, in CNR livery

The Canadian Northern Railway, was the first of the great trunk lines engineered across Canada in competition with the Canadian Pacific, developed from the enterprise of William Mackenzie, and Donald Mann, in providing originally a second line to serve the Prairies. Later it was extended 'from sea to sea', and in the west paralleled the Canadian Pacific down the canyons of the Fraser River. The 4–6–0 was its principal source of motive power, and the engine illustrated was one of a class of fifty built in 1912–13, when construction of the most westerly sections of the line was in progress. They were not very large, by North American standards, and were designed for mixed-traffic duties, having coupled wheels of 4 ft. 9 in. diameter. A larger class, with 5 ft. 3 in. coupled wheels was introduced at the same time. But to indicate the general utilisation of the 4–6–0 it can be added that no fewer than 300 were acquired by Canadian Northern between 1907 and 1913. The engine illustrated, No. 1112, was later sold to the Quebec North Shore and Labrador Railway for use during the constructional stages, and in 1962 it was donated to the Canadian Railway Historical Association for preservation in the museum at Delson, near Montreal. During its sojourn on the QNS & L it retained the original number, which dates back to its construction in 1912.

33. Southern Railway (England): 'King Arthur' class 4–6–0

The 'King Arthur' locomotives were the 'star feature', the neon lights display of a notable family of engines on the Southern Railway. They stemmed from an important change in policy made on the London and South Western Railway in 1913 after R. W. Urie had succeeded Dugald Drummond as Chief Mechanical Engineer. At a time when most British engineers were building 3- and 4-cylinder simple locomotives for the heaviest work, Urie decided upon 2-cylinders only, with all the valve gear outside and readily accessible. His 'H15' mixed traffic 4–6–0 of 1913 was followed by the 'N15' express type of 1918, and it was this latter that R. E. L. Maunsell developed into the truly great 'King Arthur' class. Maunsell's work was much more than just a finishing touch. The 'N15' class did not steam freely, and alteration had to be made to the draughting arrangements in the smokebox; but once that was done the modified engines, and the true 'King Arthurs' that followed them, showed, and sustained, brilliant form. The naming of the engines after characters in the Arthurian legend was a stroke of genius publicity-wise. Regular travellers and enthusiasts alike loved it, though the more erudite did point out that two engines had been named after the same person: *Elaine* was the *Maid of Astolat*! Our picture, of *Sir Geraint*, shows the engines as originally put into traffic, before the smoke-deflecting plates were added.

34. Pennsylvania Railroad: the 'K4' class Pacific

At the time of its introduction in 1915 the 'K4' was an outstanding locomotive in every respect. Unlike most of the American railways, the Pennsylvania developed its own strongly individual locomotive practice, constantly researching into design and performance on the stationary testing plant in Altoona Works, and by work with the dynamometer car on the road. By the year 1911 conclusion had almost been reached that the 2-cylinder simple type of locomotive, with Walschaerts valve gear outside, was the most suitable for all-round express work, and the 'K2' Pacific of that year was followed by the then tremendous 'K4' of 1915, with a tractive effort of 44,000 lb. at a time when most of the largest British locomotives did not exceed 25,000 lb. For nearly thirty years the 'K4' and no other was the standard express locomotive of the Pennsylvania: 425 of them in all, and used on some of the fastest trains in the U.S.A. On the tremendous gradients between Altoona and Pittsburgh, through the Allegheny Mountains, they were used in pairs; but elsewhere they would haul trains of 800 tons at 80 m.p.h. on level track. Some of them remained in service in New Jersey until 1958. There is no more classic example of a simple, massively built steam locomotive that could stand incessant thrashing than the Pennsylvania 'K4'.

35. Great Northern Railway (U.S.A.): Mallet articulated 2-8-8-2 freight locomotive

The original concept of an articulated locomotive by Anatole Mallet was of a compound, with the high- and low-pressure cylinders driving separate engine units. But although by the late 1920s this principle had been expanded into locomotives of colossal proportions, there was evidence then that while the general articulated principle was retained, preference was beginning to turn towards 4-cylinder layouts in which all cylinders received live steam from the boiler. The Class 'R2' Great Northern locomotive was an early example of this trend dating from 1919. It was designed for slow hard slogging on long adverse gradients – to haul a trailing load of 4,000 tons at 10 m.p.h. up a gradient of 1 in 100. Like all large Mallets of that era, they were not very stable at any speed, and they were limited to a maximum of 40 m.p.h. Interesting features to be noted are the two cross-compound air compressors of the Westinghouse brake system carried on the front of the smokebox, and the pleasing colour scheme with the boiler and cylinder cladding sheets painted a pale green. These huge engines, together with their tenders, weighed 473 tons, and had a tractive effort the highest in the world, 146,710 lb., or 65 tons.

36. Northern Railway of France: a Bréville 'super-Pacific' of 1922

After the end of the First World War the Nord developed an entirely new design of 'Pacific' engine, based on experience with various different designs, all of which were studied systematically, with the taking of indicator diagrams and other scrutinies. The Nord, also, had many more travelling inspectors than any of the other French railways, and their reports were invaluable. The new engines were de Glehn compounds, with a high degree of superheat, and a special feature was the careful proportioning of valve openings and cross-sectional areas of steam passages. The high-pressure cylinders had piston valves, while the low-pressure had balanced slide valves. As usual on the de Glehn compounds on the Nord the control of the valve gear for the high- and low-pressure cylinders was independent – leaving it to the driver's skill and experience to make the necessary adjustments. The forty engines of this design did some outstandingly fine work with the English boat trains loaded often to nearly 600 tons and conveyed at 75 m.p.h. on level track. It was a standard of performance unequalled in Europe at the time. The later development of the design under the direction of Collin, but worked out by de Caso, included a number of detail changes, and improved the maintenance record; yet the magnificent early performances of the Bréville engines were not generally surpassed.

37. Great Western Railway (England): the 'King' class 4-cylinder 4-6-0

The classic locomotive development by G. J. Churchward, at Swindon, culminated in the production by his successor, C. B. Collett, of the 'King' class of 4-cylinder 4-6-0 in 1927. Apart from the very high tractive effort of 40,300 lb. for a locomotive weighing no more than 89 tons, the basic features of the design were the 4-cylinder engine layout, similar to that of de Glehn, but non-compound; the high boiler pressure, of 250 lb. per sq. in., and the scientifically developed boiler and firebox, shaped to avoid sharp corners and tight bends in the plates, where local heating could give rise to leakage. Although expensive to construct, these boilers amply justified their first cost by their low maintenance charges. The degree of superheat was low, to avoid heat being wasted in the exhaust; but this feature, admirable in theory, was practicable only because the firemen were trained to keep boiler pressure constantly up to maximum, using proven techniques in firing the specially selected coal. The pioneer engine, No. 6000 *King George V* (now preserved in working order), represented the G.W.R. and Great Britain, at the centenary celebrations of the Baltimore and Ohio Railway in 1927. Our picture shows the engine prepared for the trip to America, fitted with the Westinghouse brake. The bell, which is now carried on the buffer beam, was presented while the engine was in America.

38. South African Railways: the Class '15F' 4–8–2 express, and fast goods locomotive

When the decision was made to standardise the 3 ft. 6 in. gauge in South Africa, railway development in the four territories that came to form the 'Union' in 1910 had scarcely passed beyond the early colonising stage. The choice was made not only because of cheapness in construction but because then it was felt that the British standard 4 ft. 8½ in. gauge was not suitable for such rugged country as that through which the line from the Cape had to force a way to reach the great inland plateaux. Speeds were of little consequence, and the famous 7th class 4–8–0 was adequate for all needs. By 1920 the situation had changed out of all recognition, and by successive upgrading of the track all traces of a light colonising railway had disappeared, and locomotives larger and heavier than any in Great Britain were running the 3 ft. 6 in. lines in South Africa. The '15F' 4–8–2, a very popular general-service unit, is a splendid example of steam locomotive construction, and no fewer than 255 are in service. They are limited to a maximum speed of

55 m.p.h., and this they quickly attain in hauling express passenger trains, while some of the freight trains they work are so long and heavy as to need *two* of these big engines. With their tenders they weigh 177¾ tons.

39. Indian broad gauge standard: 2–8–2 heavy freight locomotive, Class 'XD'

The standardisation of locomotive power on the Indian railways, begun in the early 1900s with the B.E.S.A. types, as exemplified by the Madras and Southern Mahratta 4–4–0, was carried a notable stage further in the 1920s by the production of the large 'Pacific' and 2–8–2 types. The 'XD' was the maximum power freight engine used on the majority of the broad-gauge lines. On no more than a few was the still larger and heavier 'XE' permitted. The 'XD' has proved an excellent investment. The boiler was designed to steam freely on the local coals, and many engines of the type are still in service today, nearly fifty years after their first introduction. Then they were finished in plain black, with no more adornment than the stainless-steel boiler bands and the initials of the railways to which they were allocated on their tenders. The one shown in our picture was on the South Indian Railway. Since Independence, and the grouping of the railways into geographical regions, distinctive colours have been adopted, as shown in the pictures of the present standard types. The older classes like the 'XD' have had the regional colours added, and I have seen 'XDs' at Cochin in the orange-and-black style of the present Southern Railway.

40. Bengal Nagpur Railway: 4-cylinder de Glehn compound Pacific

The Bengal Nagpur, pursuing its individual policy in locomotive practice, had derived much satisfaction from the working of some 4-cylinder de Glehn compound 'Atlantic' engines purchased from the North British Locomotive Company before the First World War. After the war, when the new Indian standard designs were being introduced elsewhere, the Bengal Nagpur made a close study of the developing French practice on the de Glehn principles, taking particular note of the outstanding performances of the Bréville 'Super-Pacifics' on the Northern

Railway. For the new Indian locomotives, which would be fired on Bengal coal, the boilers were the same as those of the 'XC' Indian standard heavy 'Pacifics', but using a pressure of 250 lb. per sq. in. instead of 180. The compound system followed closely that of the Bréville engines on the Nord, including balanced slide valves for the low-pressure cylinders. In the specification for these magnificent locomotives the tractive effort was quoted modestly at 60 per cent of boiler pressure, 28,700 lb., or not so great as a standard 'XC' Pacific. But if the more usual 85 per cent was taken, the true power could be assessed, for the tractive effort then became 40,500 lb. The total weight of engine and tender was 170·6 tons.

41. Paris–Orleans Railway: successor to the epoch-marking Pacific No. 3566

In writing of the Paris–Orleans de Glehn compound 'Atlantics' and their superb work mention was made of how the subsequent 'Pacifics' did not attain the same standards. The analysis to find out why not was made by André Chapelon, then an assistant engineer in the locomotive depart-ment at Tours. Having found where the deficiencies lay, auth-ority was given for one of the larger wheeled 'Pacifics', No. 3566, to be rebuilt. Most of the troubles lay in restricted areas through the steam passages, through the regulator, and the valves, and Lentz-type poppet valves operated by Walschaerts gear were substituted for piston valves. A much enlarged super-heater was fitted, to ensure that steam remained dry until ex-hausted from the low-pressure cylinders; a twin-orifice blast-pipe and double chimney already fitted to a number of Paris–Orleans locomotives was included in the modifications. Numerous other smaller details were changed; but the cumulative result was astounding, in that the power output was increased by fifty per cent – fifty! Syste-matic rebuilding of other engines of the class began, and as further electrification on the Orleans itself made some of the older Pacifics redundant, some of these engines were rebuilt like No. 3566 and transferred to the Nord, where they did equally magnificent work. Our picture shows one of the second batch on the Orleans Railway which had larger low-pressure cylinders and did even finer work.

42. South Australian Railways: Shea's giant 4-8-4 locomotive

The era of giant locomotives in South Australia began with a vengeance with the arrival in Adelaide in 1926 of the first of Shea's famous trio – 4-8-2, 2-8-2, and 4-6-2 – from England. The first named was of course the centre of greatest interest on arrival, and well it might have been! Never before in all railway history had there been such a staggering step-up in power. The little 'RX' 4-6-0 of 1899 vintage weighed 89 tons, with its tender, and beside this Shea's 4-8-2 weighed 213 tons, and had a tractive power $2\frac{1}{2}$ times greater. The enginemen took one look at the new giants and said they just would not go through the tunnels; but it was not long before they came to appreciate their tremendous power and reliability. Although they were expected to, and did, haul more than double the earlier loads, the fireman's task was made easier by the fitting of mechanical stokers. Even this was not enough for the enterprising management of the South Australian Railways, and to enable the load over the mountain section to be increased from

500 to 540 tons, Shea fitted his great engines with boosters. The wheel arrangement then became 4-8-4, and the tractive effort, with booster in operation, went up from 51,000 to 59,000 lb. It is in this form that our picture shows one of these engines.

43. Chinese National Railways: the Vulcan 4-8-4 of 1935

These great locomotives, twenty-four of which were built by the Vulcan Foundry Ltd. in 1935, were without question the most remarkable exported from England in the long trade in railway equipment to the Far East. The requirements were threefold: high tractive power for climbing the 1 in 70 gradients on the northern part of the Canton–Hankow Line; ability to run fast on the level; ability to steam freely on low-grade coal. The large firebox of the Wootten wide-based type had a grate area of 68 sq. ft. and a long combustion chamber extending forward into the boiler barrel. The front end was internally streamlined to give the freest possible flow of steam, and the superheater was exceptionally large. The main frames were of the bar type. To keep the large grate fed without fatigue to the fireman a mechanical stoker was included in the equipment. Six of these engines allocated to the heavily graded Canton–Hankow line had booster-driven bogies on the tenders. They proved very satisfactory engines in traffic, and can certainly be ranked among the 'great' locomotives of history.

44. New York Central: the J3a 'Hudson' 4-6-4

The New York Central, with its 'water level' route to the west, had to concentrate on hard, steady running at continuously high speed. Little in the way of hill climbing was needed, and there were no easy stretches on which one could coast downhill. Locomotives were designed to be worked at rates of steam admission that would be considered 'thrashing to death' on British and European engines. Whereas the 'Pacifics' of the London and North Eastern and of the London Midland and Scottish Railways would normally be worked with the valves cutting off at 15–20 per cent of the piston stroke when running at normal express speed, the optimum driving standard for a New York Central 'Hudson' was

57 per cent up to 56 m.p.h., 42 per cent up to 75 m.p.h., and 35 per cent right up to 85 m.p.h. And to work those heavy trains such cut-offs were certainly needed, with loads of more than 1,000 tons taken at 75 m.p.h. on level track. In the run of 403 miles between Harmon and Buffalo, 22 tons of coal were burned. The front end was finely designed to permit of the free flow of steam, and needless to say, the firebox had to be enormous. Despite the extremely hard driving necessary to keep schedules, the standard of reliability was high, and before the Second World War the 'Hudson' engines were, on an average, running 110,000 miles every year.

45. London and North Eastern Railway: the record-holding 'A4' class streamlined Pacific

The introduction of external streamlined casings on the new 'Pacifics' for the Silver Jubilee service of 1935 was a master stroke of publicity. The 'A4' class included many improvements in machinery and steam circuit over the previous non-streamlined 'A3s', and they would have been exceptionally fast engines without any external streamlining. Their initial task was the lightly loaded 'Silver Jubilee' express, run at a cruising speed on level track of 90 m.p.h.; but they also came to work on the heavy East Coast Anglo-Scottish expresses with loads of more than 500 tons, and in contrast to the severe driving of the 'Hudson' engines on the New York Central, an 'A4', cutting off at no more than 15 per cent of the piston stroke would take a 500-ton train at 75 m.p.h. on level track. Meritorious, and revenue earning though this was, the 'A4s' will be best remembered by their spectacular feats of maximum speed, at 100 m.p.h. and more. Of the 'A4s' *Mallard* holds the world record for steam traction, with 126 m.p.h., while *Silver Fox* the engine in our picture holds the British record for the highest speed ever attained with an ordinary service train, 113 m.p.h. hauling the southbound 'Silver Jubilee' express in 1936.

46. Chicago, Milwaukee, St. Paul and Pacific Railroad: streamlined 4-6-4 for the 'Hiawatha' express

The design of these striking locomotives had a basis that was somewhat analogous to that of the 'A4' Pacifics on the London and North Eastern Railway, namely that they had a dual function of hauling the very fast, relatively light 'Hiawatha' day expresses over the 410½ miles between Chicago and St. Paul that involved regular running at 100 m.p.h. and more with trains of about 400 tons, but also the haulage of heavy sleeping-car trains that at times loaded up to twenty-one cars or a gross trailing tonnage of about 1,400. Introduced in 1938, the new 4-6-4s represented some of the most advanced design practice in the U.S.A. They were built on a one-piece cast-steel 'bed' that incorporated cylinders, valve chests, smokebox saddle, and air brake reservoir all in the one casting. The unusually high boiler pressure of 300 lb. per sq. in. was used, and the huge firegrate of 96½ sq. ft. was of course fed by a mechanical stoker. The tender, having a capacity of 25 tons of coal, was, when fully loaded, not far short of the engine weight, the respective figures being 167½ and 185¼ tons. The total weight of engine and tender, 352¾ tons, was needed to work a train of 430 tons at the speed scheduled for the 'Hiawatha'. On test one of these engines covered a stretch of 5 miles at 120 m.p.h.

47. Canadian Pacific Railway: the 'Royal Hudson' 4-6-4 locomotive

On the Canadian Pacific Railway the introduction of the 4-6-4 type was largely dictated by the severe competition that developed with the Canadian National for the prestige inter-city traffic between Montreal and Toronto, around 1930. The trains were heavy, and the schedules were progressively cut, and just as the New York Central adopted the 4-6-4 type for its 'water-level' route, so the CPR did the same. By 1931 the company had the fastest start-to-stop run in the whole world: 124 miles between Smith's Falls and Montreal West in 108 minutes, 68·9 m.p.h. Going west the timing was nearly as fast, and with loads of 600–700 tons. The first class of 'Hudsons', the '2800' series, made these runs, and it was a development of them, the '2850' class, that took the road in 1937. Like the original class of 1929, they were all built by the Montreal Locomotive Works, and it was No. 2850 that was selected to haul the Royal Train on the C.P.R. during the tour of King George VI and Queen Elizabeth in 1939. Our picture shows this engine in the special blue and silver livery applied for this occasion. Big though the 'Royal Hudsons' of the CPR were, their total weight, with tender, was 288 tons, considerably less than the 'Hiawatha' 4-6-4s of the Milwaukee.

48. Great Southern Railways (Ireland): the 3-cylinder 4-6-0 express locomotive *Maeve*

The year 1939 saw the completion of the largest and most powerful steam locomotive type ever to run in Ireland, the 3-cylinder 4-6-0 *Maeve* of the Great Southern Railways. The former GS & WR had at one time been a source of enterprising locomotive development, but since the 1920s with the constraint of economic conditions, no new designs had appeared, and the moderate powered 2-cylinder 4-6-0s had been carrying on. There was certainly a need for something larger, and the new design of 1939 was a notable advance. In general proportions it could be likened to the 'Royal Scots' of the LMSR; but there were certain important differences. Although having a double chimney, there was not a twin-orifice blast pipe of the usual kind; the one inside cylinder exhausted up the leading chimney and the two outside cylinders through the after one. The Belpaire firebox was carefully shaped in the Great Western style, and every detail had been worked out afresh. There was little opportunity to see what the new engines could do before war came in September 1939; but a return trip from Dublin to Cork and back in the last fortnight of peace gave me some impressive results. The other two engines of the class were named *Macha* and *Tailte*.

49. Atchison, Topeka, and Santa Fé: a '3765' class 4-8-4

If, in the heyday of steam locomotive operation, one had been asked to name some of the most strenuous of all duties those allocated to the Santa Fé, '3765' 4-8-4s would immediately come to mind. The 'Chief', for example, on which one locomotive worked through over the 1,234 miles between La Junta and Los Angeles had to cross three successive mountain passes at 7,622, 7,437, and 7,335 ft. above sea level; dip down to the valleys between, at speeds often touching 100 m.p.h. and all with

a train often loaded to fifteen or sixteen cars – American style cars too! And this one engine was handled by *nine* different crews in the course of the journey, on stages varying between 105 and 167 miles. The '3765' class, built by the Baldwin Locomotive Works, date from 1937. Like all American giants of the final steam era, they were straightforward 2-cylinder simples, with everything needing attention outside. Their proportions were enormous: pressure 300 lb. per sq. in.; cylinders 28 in. diameter by 32 in. stroke; tractive effort 66,000 lb. They were oil-fired, and their tanks, carrying 7,000 gallons, were replenished at one or more of the stopping stations. It was a case of brute strength, but a built-in strength based on nigh a hundred years of locomotive constructional experience.

50. German State Railways (Reichsbahn): the Series '52' Austerity war locomotive

Standardisation of locomotive power was a point of major policy of the Reichsbahn in the years between the two world wars. While much was being done to encourage and develop spectacular passenger services like the diesel-electric railcar 'Flying Hamburger', and its successors, steam remained the backbone of the freight service, and from the successful heavy freight 2–10–0 of Series '44' there was introduced, in 1939, a lightweight version, Series '50', that would have a greatly increased route availability. Then as war conditions were intensified, and large numbers of additional locomotives were needed, constructed, moreover, in the most economical fashion, the 'Austerity' version Series '52' was produced. Already the series '50' was a very powerful engine for its weight, having a tractive effort of 50,000 lb. from an 85-ton locomotive; no less than 26 tons was saved on the total weight of engine and tender, because the '52' weighed only 117 tons, against the 144 tons of the '50'. Everything conceivable was omitted, like smoke-deflecting plates, running boards, feed-water heaters, and all refinements. More than 10,000 of them were built during the war, but on the many that remain today may be seen the restoration of some at least of the fittings that were considered not absolutely essential in wartime.

51. French National Railways (SNCF): the 141 R 2–8–2: L'Américaine

French locomotive practice had, almost from the beginning of railways, been highly specialised and individualistic; but at the end of the Second World War the situation was such that, to use a colloquialism, one could not be choosey. New locomotives were needed desperately, and the '141 R' was obtained in large quantities from North America. It was utterly different from anything that had previously run in France – a simple, hard-slogging, 2-cylinder machine, completely devoid of the various sophistications that had distinguished French locomotives for so long. It proved not only a godsend but also, astonishingly, a very popular locomotive. Balanced in the old way, it was rather heavy-handed on the track, and had to be limited to 100 km/hr. (62 m.p.h.) in consequence. But in those immediate post-war days speed did not matter. It was hard, solid reliability that counted. Of the 1,340 locomotives actually built, 1,323 went into service in France, seventeen being lost at sea when the ship foundered in a gale. By 1948 the 1,323 engines were responsible for one-third of the total train mileage on the SNCF, and for no less than 49 per cent of the total ton-miles worked – an astonishing record for a truly great locomotive class.

52. Indian Railways: the new standard express passenger 4–6–2, type 'WP'

Following experience with the various standard locomotive designs introduced in the years between the two world wars, the Indian railways worked out new designs for both 4–6–2 passenger and 2–8–2 goods to be introduced generally on all the broad-gauge lines, now completely unified in administration since the granting of Independence. The first of the new 'Pacifics' were built in North America, while the 2–8–2s were built in Great Britain. Although having a semi-streamlined exterior, the 'Pacific' was a very simple, straightforward 2-cylinder design that provided a tractive effort of 30,600 lb. Few of the Indian trunk routes then permitted speeds in excess of 60 m.p.h., and the new design was an admirable one for working the heavy mail and long-distance passenger trains, with a minimum of day-to-day mainten-

ance. The locomotives use the indigenous coals, and usually two firemen are carried, sharing the work of firing and other footplate duties between them. With the establishment of the territorial regions, distinctive colours were adopted, and the engine in our picture carries the style of the Central Railway, the successor to the Great Indian Peninsular Railway. In the cab the engine shown has a special decoration over the firehole door, appropriate to its working of the Taj Express daily between New Delhi and Agra – a very popular service with tourists.

53. Canadian Pacific Railway: the 'Selkirk' 2–10–4 for Rocky Mountain service

Between Calgary, Alberta, and Revelstoke, British Columbia, lies what is probably the most severe section of trunk main-line railway to be found anywhere in the world. It passes through two great mountain ranges: the great *massif* of the Rockies, between Calgary and Field, and then the Selkirk Range, with a summit level in the Connaught Tunnel, following the ascent of the formidable Beaver Hill. Although freight-train loads are now much heavier, it is enough to say that with maximum tonnage trains *thirteen* diesel-electric locomotives of 3,000 horsepower are now required on the Beaver Hill. The 2–10–4 type, aptly known as the 'Selkirks', was introduced on the CPR in 1929, and although these enormous engines had a tractive effort of 78,000 lb., it needed four of them – two in front and two in rear – to get the heaviest trains of those days, 2,000 tons, up the Beaver Hill. The later 'Selkirks', with the semi-streamlined exterior, began to take up their duties in 1938. The sixteen engines of the '5920' class represent the ultimate in Rocky Mountain steam power, and one of them, No. 5934 is preserved and on display in Mewata Park, Calgary. The sister engine, No. 5935, in the museum of the Canadian Railway Historical Association at Delson, near Montreal, was the very last standard-gauge steam locomotive built for a Canadian railway.

54. South African Railways: the 'GMAM' Beyer-Garratt 4–8–2 + 2–8–4 locomotive

Ever since the successful trials of the 'GA' locomotive on the Natal main line soon after the First World War the 'Beyer-Garratt' type became firmly established in South Africa, and some very large and powerful units had been supplied by the year 1939. The last had been the 'GM' class, with the 4–8–2 + 2–8–4 wheel arrangement, designed for the Krugersdorp–Mafeking line to do the work that formerly needed two 4–8–2 ordinary tender engines of Class 19D. After the war this particular category of Garratt was greatly multiplied, with no more than slight modifications. The latest of these, the 'GMAM' shown in our picture, claims a special distinction. In 1955 when there was an urgent need for more locomotives Messrs. Beyer, Peacock & Co. were offered a contract for thirty-five of these great engines on condition that delivery should commence in seven months – on the face of it an almost impossible task. But by a tremendous co-operative effort the first engine was steamed in *six* months. They have a tractive effort of 68,800 lb., and to provide ample water supplies on the long runs through what is near-desert country an auxiliary water tank is carried, seen in our picture beyond the forward engine unit. In service it is usual to work these locomotives with the cab end leading. Construction of the 'GM' series of Garratts continued until 1958, by which time 136 were in traffic.

55. Pennsylvania Railroad: the 'T1' 4-4-4-4 non-articulated high-speed locomotive of 1942

The standard of performance aimed at in the design of the remarkable 'T1' class non-articulated locomotive was the haulage of trains of 1,000 tons, at 100 m.p.h. on level track, and it is interesting to compare this unusual type with the conventional 4-8-4 of the Santa Fé, illustrated earlier in this book. Both have an almost identical tractive effort, but because of a smaller boiler the Pennsylvania engine has a lower potential maximum horsepower of 4,627 as compared with 5,344 in the Santa Fé. There is, however, a considerable difference in the service, as the Pennsylvania 4-4-4-4 was intended for the level stretches west of Pittsburgh; the Santa Fé 4-8-4, as described earlier, had to take everything in its stride between Kansas City and Los Angeles. The choice of two independent four-coupled engines gave the Pennsylvania 4-4-4-4 better balancing, from smaller cylinders and

the divided drive, and in actual service the design target was fully achieved. Their life was, however, relatively short. From their introduction in 1942 it was not many years before the onset of the diesel-electric was experienced in all its intensity, and not a great deal is known as to how the initial success of these engines could be sustained, year in, year out. The total weight of engine and tender was 461 tons, including the exceptional coal-carrying capacity of $37\frac{1}{2}$ tons.

56. Japanese National Railways: the 'C 62' class 4-6-4 express passenger locomotive

The steam locomotive stock of the Japanese National Railways is classified according to the number of coupled axles. Thus all six-coupled engines have the prefix 'C'; all eight-coupled 'D', and so on, no matter what the actual wheel arrangement is. Among the 'Cs' one finds 2-6-0, 2-6-2, 4-6-2, and 4-6-4. The English and American numerology is used in preference to the European, so that a 'Pacific' is a 4-6-2 in Japan, not a 2-3-1, and the English numerals are actually used, as everywhere in Japan, because of their greater simplicity than the indigenous system of figures. The 'C 62' is the largest and most powerful passenger locomotive ever to run in Japan, and from its massive, functional, highly modern appearance one could well imagine it could rank beside some of the giant American 4-6-4s. But of course it was designed for the 3 ft. 6 in. gauge, without the freedom of loading gauge that enabled such huge engines to be put on the road in South Africa, and the 'C 62' is a relatively small, though a very fine engine. Its weight, without tender, is only 87¼ tons, or less than the Great Western *King George V*, and has a tractive effort of 30,583 lb. The twenty engines of this class did excellent work, especially on the heavily graded route between Hakodate and Sapporo, on the island of Hokkaido.

57. Union Pacific Railroad: the 4-8-8-4 express freight locomotive of 1941 – 'Big Boy'

The Union Pacific Railroad has the distinction of having operated the largest and heaviest steam locomotives ever built. By the mid-1930s the problem of getting stable riding at express speed on a Mallet articulated locomotive had been largely overcome, by

an even weight distribution between the front and back engine units, front boiler support with flat bearing surfaces, and use of a four-wheeled bogie at the leading end. In a class of 4-6-6-4 engines built for the Union Pacific by the American Locomotive Company (ALCO) the stability in riding was such that they could safely be run up to 70 m.p.h. But the Union Pacific needed still larger engines to haul the heaviest express freight trains over the Wasatch Mountains, between Green River, Wyoming, and Ogden, Utah, where the ruling gradient is 1 in 88. Thus came the 'Big Boys'. These enormous locomotives weighed 340 tons without their tenders, which latter weighed another 194 tons. They had a tractive effort of 135,375 lb., and used to work the priority express fruit trains, which were limited to a maximum of seventy refrigerated box cars, a load of about 3,200 tons. With these trains the speed was often around 80 m.p.h. There were, however, other duties that involved much heavier loads, and in climbing the 1 in 67 gradient of Sherman Hill, Wyoming, it was not unusual to see a pair of these giant locomotives on one train.

58. British Railways : London Midland Region – the 'Duchess' class 4–6–2 locomotive

British railway enthusiasts will never cease to debate upon which was the finest type of steam express passenger locomotive ever to run in Great Britain; but while there are many angles from which the claims of the various contestants could be considered, in one respect of simple fact the 'Duchess' class Pacifics of Sir William Stanier stands first. During scientifically conducted dynamometer car trials on the Settle and Carlisle line engine No. 46225 *Duchess of Gloucester* sustained for half an hour the highest rate of evaporation in the boiler ever reached by a British steam locomotive, in hauling an equivalent load of 900 tons up 'The Long Drag', 1 in 100 for 17 miles between Settle Junction and Blea Moor at a steady 30 m.p.h. The 'Duchesses' were, of course, high-speed express locomotives and hauled trains of 500 tons at speeds up to 85 m.p.h. on level track. The engine shown in our picture, the *Duchess of Rutland*, was one of those built in 1938, and streamlined. This external casing was removed soon after the war, and then there began a series of different liveries: first black; then the British Railways blue; next a change to dark green, and finally a reversion to something similar to the LMS 'Derby red', but with the British Railways insignia on the tender. The 'Duchess' class had a tractive effort of 40,000 lb. and the weight of engine only was $105\frac{1}{4}$ tons.

59. Canadian National Railways : the restored 4–8–2 locomotive No. 6060

The Canadian National Railway organisation, consolidated finally in January 1923 when the Grand Trunk Railway was taken over, placed orders at once for large new 4–8–2 locomotives. While the rival Canadian Pacific advanced from the 4–6–2 to the 4–6–4 'CN' henceforth used nothing but eight-coupled express locomotives on its heaviest duties. The first 4–8–4s followed in 1927, and all these engines were finished in a utilitarian, workaday black, except for five special high-speed units having 6 ft. 8 in. coupled wheels instead of the usual 6 ft. 1 in. Then after a long series of 4–8–4s the Montreal Locomotive Works in 1944 built the twenty engines of the 'U-i-f' class, 4–8–2s of quite distinctive appearance. This was all the more remarkable because at that time the restrictions of war were stripping most of the glamour from railway operation. The new engines 6060–6079 were most handsomely styled, and included quite an amount of *colour*. When the time came for the diesels to supersede steam three of these engines were preserved: 6060 at Jasper, 6069 at Sarnia, and 6077 at Capreol. One of the big 4–8–4s had been maintained in running condition, and when the time came for this latter engine to need extensive repairs, arrangements were made to exchange her, as a static exhibit, with the 4–8–2 No. 6060, and this engine, to the delight of all Canadian enthusiasts, is now available 'in glorious technicolor' for working special steam-hauled trains.

60. Rhodesia Railways: the '15A' class 4–6–4 + 4–6–4 Beyer-Garratt locomotive

On a railway system such as that of Rhodesia there is every advantage in having large main-line locomotives capable of hand-ling any kind of traffic. For while it was desirable to run the mail trains at the maximum speed possible on the 3 ft. 6 in. gauge lines, it was equally necessary to obtain maximum utilisation of locomotives. On the long through runs manning is on the caboose system, with two crews alternately working and resting. The introduction of the splendid '15' and '15A' classes of Beyer-Garratt loco-motive, with their versatility in traffic, enabled duty rosters to be arranged working outward on a freight train and returning on one of the mails. These locomotives, with the 4–6–4 + 4–6–4 wheel arrangement have proved positive greyhounds on the 3 ft. 6 in. gauge, running easily up to 55 m.p.h. with passenger and mail trains of 500–650 tons, and yet equally capable of dealing with 1,000-ton freights – naturally at slower speed. There are now no fewer than seventy-four of the '15' series Garratts in service in Rhodesia; thirty-four of these form the original 15th class, first in-troduced in 1940, and having a boiler pressure of 180 lb. per sq. in. The remaining forty represent the more powerful '15A' class, with 200 lb. pressure. The tractive effort of the '15A' is 41,908 lb., from a locomotive weighing 186¾ tons in working order.

61. East African Railways: the '59' class 4–8–2 + 2–8–4 Beyer-Garratt locomotive

The former Kenya and Uganda Railway first began to use the Beyer-Garratt type of locomotive in the 1930s, when the light nature of the track precluded the use of any greater axle load than 11¾ tons on the greater part of the main line. On the branches, some of which had heavy traffic, the maximum axle load was only 10 tons. It was in these circumstances that motive power was developed up to the remarkable 4–8–4 + 4–8–4 locomotives of Class EC3, having a tractive effort of 46,100 lb. These were confined to sections where 11¾-ton axle loads were permitted. In the years following the Second World War traffic developed to such an extent between Nairobi and Mombasa that freight trains had to be made up to 1,200 tons, and on long gradients of 1 in 50 the 'EC3' locomotives could not cope, and smaller Garratts were used in pairs. With this experience, however, it became clear that the track could withstand far heavier axle loads, and the way was clear for the colossal '59' class, the most powerful engines ever put on to the metre gauge, with the 4–8–2 + 2–8–4 wheel arrangement, a tractive effort of 83,500 lb. and a total weight in working order of 251¾ tons. Thirty-four of these engines handle the entire freight traffic between Nairobi and the coast, in train loads of 1,000–1,200 tons. If one of them is not available *two* diesel-electric locomotives are needed to work the same trains.

62. Japanese National Railways: the 'C 57' class light Pacific locomotive

In the general scheme of locomotive modernisation undertaken in the 1930s the 'C 57' Pacific, although one of the later designs to be introduced, was cast for an important role. There were many lines where more powerful locomotives were needed, but where track conditions did not permit a higher axle load than 14 tons. The 'C 57' was built with the remarkably high tractive effort of 28,268 lb. These locomotives have a very free steaming boiler, although the coal used is of very low grade and makes a tremendous amount of smoke. The blastpipes are surrounded by a fine gauze filter to prevent too much unburnt matter from being thrown out in the exhaust. These little engines, though of such high power, are used on passenger and freight trains alike on the lesser routes. An interesting instance that I saw personally, and which inspired our picture was that of engine No. C57-117 on the southern island of Kyushu, working the Royal Train for the Emperor of Japan one day, and a freight train on the very next day. The total weight of these engines is 68 tons, without tender – a great little engine nevertheless.

63. Indian Railways: the 'YG' standard metre gauge 2-8-2 freight engine

Since the end of the Second World War a policy of general standardisation of steam motive power has been adopted on the Indian Railways, and new construction either at the Chittaranjan Works or by contractors has been generally limited to four major designs, two each for the broad and the metre gauge; and in each case 4–6–2 for passenger and 2–8–2 for freight. The metre gauge classes 'YP' and 'YG' have the same boiler, but the former has 4 ft. 6 in. coupled wheels, and $15\frac{1}{4}$ in. by 24 in. cylinders, while the 'YG' has 4 ft.

o in. coupled wheels and $16\frac{1}{4}$ in. by 24 in. cylinders. Construction of both classes began in 1949, in Great Britain, and so far as the 'YG' was concerned such was the urgent need for new metre-gauge goods engines that orders were placed in Austria, Czecho-Slovakia, and Japan, in addition to many being built in India, both by contract and at the Indian Railways works at Chittaranjan. The very last steam locomotives built in India were a batch of 100 of the 'YG' class, completed early in 1972, by which time the class numbered well over 1,000 engines. The adding of the regional colours has been extended to these metre-gauge standard locomotives, and our picture shows one in the colours of the Southern Railway.

64. British Railways: the last steam locomotive built, the '9F' 2-10-0 *Evening Star*

There is always not a little sadness at the ending of an epoch, and when the big standard 2–10–0 *Evening Star* emerged from the erecting shops at Swindon in 1960 it was the end of a story that had continued for 154 years, ever since Richard Trevithick ran his famous tram-engine on the plateway at Penydarran in 1804. In the period from 1942 onwards the British steam locomotive had passed through some vicissitudes as well as some triumphs, and on this account it is all the pleasanter to recall that the last locomotive built belonged to a class that can unqualifyingly be set down as great – very great. The '9F' was designed as a heavy freight engine. There had been strong pressure from senior assistants to make it a 2–8–2; but R. A. Riddles, who was then Member of the Railway Executive for Mechanical Engineering, was unshaken and specified a 2–10–0. Perhaps the most astonishing feature of the working of these fine engines was their versatility. Freight engines they certainly were, but they could run like stags, and more than one instance has been fully authenticated of a maximum speed of 90 m.p.h. Sadly their life was short, not because of any weakness in design or construction, but because British Railways decided precipitately to replace steam by diesels and electrics regardless of whether or not the existing power had reached the end of its economc life.

INDEX